Readings in Literary Criticism 1

CRITICS ON KEATS

Readings in Literary Criticism

CRITICS ON KEATS

Readings in Literary Criticism

Edited by Judith O'Neill

University of Miami Press
Coral Gables, Florida

ACKNOWLEDGMENTS

Kenneth Allott: from *John Keats: A Reassessment*, ed. by Kenneth Muir. Reprinted by permission of Liverpool University Press, Liverpool. This essay was originally published in *Essays in Criticism*, vol. VI, no. 3, 1956.

W. Jackson Bate: from *The Major English Romantic Poets: A Symposium in Reappraisal*, ed. by Clarence D. Thorpe, Carlos Baker, and Bennett Weaver. Copyright © 1957 by Southern Illinois University Press. Reprinted by permission of the publisher.

Bernard Blackstone: from *The Consecrated Urn*. Reprinted by permission of Longmans, Green & Co., Ltd., London.

Cleanth Brooks: from *The Well Wrought Urn*. Copyright 1947 by Cleanth Brooks. Reprinted by permission of Harcourt, Brace & World, Inc., New York.

John Holloway: from *The Cambridge Journal*, vol. V, April, 1952. Reprinted by permission of Bowes & Bowes Ltd., London.

D. G. James: from *The Romantic Comedy*. Reprinted by permission of Oxford University Press, London.

F. R. Leavis: from *Revaluation: Tradition and Development in English Poetry*. Copyright 1947 by George W. Stewart, Publisher, Inc., New York. Reprinted by permission of Chatto & Windus Ltd., London. This essay originally appeared in *Scrutiny*, vol. IV, March, 1936.

Kenneth Muir: from *John Keats: A Reassessment*, ed. by Kenneth Muir. Reprinted by permission of Liverpool University Press, Liverpool. This essay was first published in *Essays in Criticism*, vol. II, no. 1, 1952.

John Middleton Murry: Reprinted with the permission of Farrar, Straus & Giroux, Inc., from *Keats*, by J. Middleton Murry. Printed in the United States in 1955.

E. C. Pettet: from *On the Poetry of John Keats*. Reprinted by permission of Cambridge University Press, London.

Roger Sharrock: from *A Review of English Literature*, ed. by A. Norman Jeffares, vol. II, no. 1, January, 1961. Reprinted by permission of the author.

Lionel Trilling: Reprinted with the permission of Farrar, Straus & Giroux, Inc., from *The Selected Letters of John Keats*, ed. by Lionel Trilling. Copyright 1951 by Lionel Trilling.

Aileen Ward: from *John Keats: The Making of a Poet*. Copyright © 1963 by Aileen Ward. All rights reserved. Reprinted by permission of The Viking Press, Inc.

CONTENTS

JOHN GIBSON LOCKHART

The Cockney School
of Poetry

OF all the manias of this mad age, the most incurable, as well as the most common, seems to be no other than the *Metromanie*. The just celebrity of Robert Burns and Miss Baillie has had the melancholy effect of turning the heads of we know not how many farm-servants and unmarried ladies; our very footmen compose tragedies, and there is scarcely a superannuated governess in the island that does not leave a roll of lyrics behind her in her band-box. To witness the disease of any human understanding, however feeble, is distressing; but the spectacle of an able mind reduced to a state of insanity is of course ten times more afflicting. It is with such sorrow as this that we have contemplated the case of Mr John Keats. This young man appears to have received from nature talents of an excellent, perhaps even of a superior order—talents which, devoted to the purposes of any useful profession, must have rendered him a respectable, if not an eminent citizen. His friends, we understand, destined him to the career of medicine, and he was bound apprentice some years ago to a worthy apothecary in town. But all has been undone by a sudden attack of the malady to which we have alluded. . . . The phrenzy of the *Poems* was bad enough in its way; but it did not alarm us half so seriously as the calm, settled, imperturbable drivelling idiocy of *Endymion*.

His Endymion is not a Greek shepherd, loved by a Grecian goddess; he is merely a young Cockney rhymester, dreaming a phantastic dream at the full of the moon. Costume, were it worth while to notice such a trifle, is violated in every page of this goodly octavo. From his prototype Hunt, John Keats has acquired a sort of vague idea, that the Greeks were a most tasteful people, and that no mythology can be so finely adapted for the purposes of poetry as theirs. It is amusing to see what a hand the two Cockneys make of this mythology; the one confesses that he never read the Greek Tragedians, and the other knows Homer only from Chapman; and both of them write about

Apollo, Pan, Nymphs, Muses, and Mysteries, as might be expected from persons of their education.... *Endymion* has just as much to do with Greece as it has with 'old Tartary the fierce'; no man, whose mind has ever been imbued with the smallest knowledge or feeling of classical history, could have stooped to profane and vulgarise every association in the manner which has been adopted by this 'son of promise'.... We venture to make one small prophecy, that his bookseller will not a second time venture £50 upon any thing he can write. It is a better and a wiser thing to be a starved apothecary than a starved poet; so back to the shop Mr John, back to 'plasters, pills, and ointment boxes', &c. But, for Heaven's sake, young Sangrado, be a little more sparing of extenuatives and soporifics in your practice than you have been in your poetry.

From *Blackwood's Edinburgh Magazine*, vol. III., no. XVII, August 1818, pp. 519–24. This article has been abridged. It was one of a series written anonymously by 'Z', who was later proved to be John Gibson Lockhart.

... I compare human life to a large Mansion of Many Apartments, two of which I can only describe, the doors of the rest being as yet shut upon me—The first we step into we call the infant or thoughtless Chamber, in which we remain as long as we do not think—We remain there a long while, and notwithstanding the doors of the second Chamber remain wide open, showing a bright appearance, we care not to hasten to it; but are at length imperceptibly impelled by the awakening of the thinking principle—within us—we no sooner get into the second Chamber, which I shall call the Chamber of Maiden-Thought, than we become intoxicated with the light and the atmosphere, we see nothing but pleasant wonders, and think of delaying there for ever in delight: However among the effects this breathing is father of is that tremendous one of sharpening one's vision into the heart and nature of Man—of convincing ones nerves that the World is full of Misery and Heartbreak, Pain, Sickness and oppression—whereby This Chamber of Maiden Thought becomes gradually darken'd and at the same time on all sides of it many doors are set open—but all dark—all leading to dark passages—We see not the ballance of good and evil. We are in a Mist—We are now in that state —We feel the 'burden of the Mystery', To this point was Wordsworth come, as far as I can conceive when he wrote 'Tintern Abbey' and it seems to me that his Genius is explorative of those dark Passages. Now if we live, and go on thinking, we too shall explore them. ...

(John Keats to J. H. Reynolds, May 3, 1818)

JOHN CROKER

Endymion: A Poetic Romance by John Keats

REVIEWERS have been sometimes accused of not reading the works which they affected to criticise. On the present occasion we shall anticipate the author's complaint, and honestly confess that we have not read his work. Not that we have been wanting in our duty—far from it—indeed, we have made efforts almost as superhuman as the story itself appears to be, to get through it; but with the fullest stretch of our perseverance, we are forced to confess that we have not been able to struggle beyond the first of the four books in which this Poetic Romance consists. We should extremely lament this want of energy, or whatever it may be, on our parts, were it not for one consolation—namely, that we are no better aquainted with the meaning of the book through which we have so painfully toiled, than we are with that of the three which we have not looked into.

It is not that Mr Keats ... has not powers of language, rays of fancy, and gleams of genius—he has all these; but he is unhappily a disciple of the new school of what has been somewhere called Cockney poetry; which may be defined to consist of the most incongruous ideas in the most uncouth language. . . . We now present [our readers] with some of the new words with which, in imitation of Mr Leigh Hunt, he adorns our language.

We are told that 'turtles *passion* their voices', that 'an arbour was *nested*', and a lady's locks '*gordian'd* up'; and to supply the place of the nouns thus verbalized Mr Keats, with great fecundity, spawns new ones; such as 'men-slugs and human *serpentry*'; the '*honey-feel* of bliss'; 'wives prepare *needments*',—and so forth.

Then he has formed new verbs by the process of cutting off their natural tails, the adverbs, and affixing them to their foreheads; thus, 'the wine out-sparkled'; the 'multitude up-followed'; and 'night up-took'. 'The wind up-blows'; and the 'hours are down-sunken'.

But if he sinks some adverbs in the verbs he compensates the language with adverbs and adjectives which he separates from the parent stock. Thus, a lady 'whispers *pantingly* and close', makes '*hushing* signs', and steers her skiff into a '*ripply* cove'; a shower falls '*refreshfully*'; and a vulture has a '*spreaded* tail'. . . . If any one should be bold enough to purchase this 'Poetic Romance', and so much more patient, than ourselves, as to get beyond the first book, and so much more fortunate as to find a meaning, we entreat him to make us acquainted with his success; we shall then return to the task which we now abandon in despair, and endeavour to make all due amends to Mr Keats and to our readers.

From *The Quarterly Review*, vol. XIX, no. XXXVII, 1818, pp. 204–8. The article has been considerably abridged.

. . . *I begin to get a little acquainted with my own strength and weakness.—Praise or blame has but a momentary effect on the man whose love of beauty in the abstract makes him a severe critic on his own Works. My own domestic criticism has given me pain without comparison beyond what Blackwood or the [Edinburgh] Quarterly could possibly inflict. and also when I feel I am right, no external praise can give me such a glow as my own solitary reperception & ratification of what is fine. J.S. is perfectly right in regard to the slipshod Endymion. That it is so is no fault of mine.—No!—though it may sound a little paradoxical. It is as good as I had power to make it— by myself—Had I been nervous about its being a perfect piece, & with that view asked advice, & trembled over every page, it would not have been written; for it is not in my nature to fumble—I will write independently.—I have written independently without Judgment—I may write independently & with judgment hereafter.—The Genius of Poetry must work out its own salvation in a man: It cannot be matured by law & precept, but by sensation & watchfulness in itself—That which is creative must create itself—In Endymion, I leaped headlong into the Sea, and thereby have become better acquainted with the Soundings, the quicksands, & the rocks, than if I had (stayed) stayed upon the green shore, and piped a silly pipe, and took tea & comfortable advice.—I was never afraid of failure; for I would sooner fail than not be among the greatest. . . .*

(John Keats to J. A. Hessey, October 8, 1818)

MATTHEW ARNOLD

John Keats

.... THE thing to be seized is that Keats had flint and iron in him, that he had character; that he was, as his brother George says, 'as much like the Holy Ghost as *Johnny Keats*,'—as that imagined sensuous weakling, the delight of the literary circles of Hampstead.... But indeed nothing is more remarkable in Keats than his clear-sightedness, his lucidity; and lucidity is in itself akin to character and to high and severe work. In spite, therefore, of his overpowering feeling for beauty, in spite of his sensuousness, in spite of his facility, in spite of his gift of expression, Keats could say resolutely : —

'I know nothing, I have read nothing; and I mean to follow Solomon's directions : "Get learning, get understanding." There is but one way for me. The road lies through application, study, and thought. I will pursue it.' ...

The truth is that 'the yearning passion for the Beautiful', which was with Keats, as he himself truly says, the master-passion, is not a passion of the sensuous or sentimental man, is not a passion of the sensuous or sentimental poet. It is an intellectual and spiritual passion. It is 'connected and made one', as Keats declares that in his case it was, 'with the ambition of the intellect'. It is, as he again says, 'the mighty *abstract idea* of Beauty in all things.' And in his last days Keats wrote : 'If I should die, I have left no immortal work behind me—nothing to make my friends proud of my memory; but I have loved the principle of beauty in all things, and if I had had time I would have made myself remembered.' He *has* made himself remembered, and remembered as no merely sensuous poet could be; and he has done it by having 'loved the principle of beauty in all things'.

For to see things in their beauty is to see things in their truth, and Keats knew it. 'What the Imagination seizes as Beauty must be Truth,' he says in prose; and in immortal verse he has said the same thing—

'Beauty is truth, truth beauty,—that is all
Ye know on earth, and all ye need to know.'

No, it is not all; but it is true, deeply true, and we have deep need to know it. And with beauty goes not only truth, joy goes with her also; and this too Keats saw and said, as in the famous first line of his *Endymion* it stands written—

'A thing of beauty is a joy for ever.'

It is no small thing to have so loved the principle of beauty as to perceive the necessary relation of beauty with truth, and of both with joy. . . .

But he had terrible bafflers—consuming disease and early death. . . . Nevertheless, let and hindered as he was, and with a short term and imperfect experience,—'young', as he says of himself, 'and writing at random, straining after particles of light in the midst of a great darkness, without knowing the bearing of any one assertion, of any one opinion',—notwithstanding all this, by virtue of his feeling for beauty and of his perception of the vital connection of beauty with truth, Keats accomplished so much in poetry, that in one of the two great modes by which poetry interprets, in the faculty of naturalistic interpretation, in what we call natural magic, he ranks with Shakespeare. 'The tongue of Kean,' he says in an admirable criticism of that great actor and of his enchanting elocution, 'the tongue of Kean must seem to have robbed the Hybla bees and left them honeyless. There is an indescribable *gusto* in his voice;—in *Richard*, "Be stirring with the lark to-morrow, gentle Norfolk!" comes from him as through the morning atmosphere towards which he yearns.' This magic, this 'indescribable *gusto* in the voice', Keats himself, too, exhibits in his poetic expression. No one else in English poetry, save Shakespeare, has in expression quite the fascinating felicity of Keats, his perfection of loveliness. 'I think,' he said humbly, 'I shall be among the English poets after my death.' He is; he is with Shakespeare.

From *Essays in Criticism, Second Series*, Macmillan and Co., London and New York, 1888, pp. 100–21. (Reprinted from Ward's English Poets, vol. IV. 1880.) Only a few excerpts from the original essay are given here.

AILEEN WARD

Keats and Tradition

... THE spread of Keats's influence on Victorian poetry ended by making him a symbol of the poet which the new talents of the 1910's and 1920's were determined to repudiate. The Victorians had fastened on the more imitable and less valuable aspects of Keats's work, his sensuousness without his objectivity, his melancholy without his 'knowledge of light and shade'. Our sense of Keats has changed; yet what now seems most significant in his art—the sureness of ear and firmness of structure, the dialectic of imagery, the tragic vision of life—remains a lesson which every poet must learn for himself.

Nevertheless, Keats's work has survived better than that of any of his contemporaries the long devaluation of romantic poetry that began about the time of Auden's appearance on the scene. Eliot has paid tribute to the Shakespearean quality of Keats's greatness, especially as it appears in his letters; and his best poems have stood up well under the most rigorous analysis of recent criticism. When these critical assessments are added to the evaluation of Keats in recent scholarship —those focused on his interest in ideas, his concern with technique, his absorption in the whole range of the English language and the whole tradition of English poetry—his place in the tradition begins to be seen more clearly. Each new discovery about his life helps disprove Byron's quip that he was 'snuffed out by an article', or indeed by anything else than tuberculosis, and to reveal him as a man uniquely gifted with the stamina needed to translate the vision of poetry into performance. ... as Middleton Murry put it, what Keats achieved in four years against heavy disadvantages can only be described as a miracle. ...

Yet it is more than a miracle. It is a fact of poetic growth which can be traced step by arduous step through Keats's poems and letters, where he may be watched laboriously reshaping the language and the sensibility he inherited into an instrument adequate to his own ideal of poetry and his own vision of human experience; it is a living proof of that continual interanimation of tradition and original talent which is the life force of poetry. In an age in which, by its best critics at least,

originality was exalted far above tradition, Keats's special originality
was his sense of dedication to the whole tradition of English poetry
and his attempt to recover it for the use of poetry in his time. And, as
Eliot has said, 'Tradition cannot be inherited; if you want it you must
obtain it by great labour.' Keats earned his place in the tradition of
English poetry by his courage to take the great dare of self-creation,
his willingness to accept failure and move beyond it, his patience in
learning his craft from those who could teach him. His sober prophecy
as he started *Hyperion*—'I think I shall be among the English Poets
after my death'—has been fulfilled; as Matthew Arnold confirmed it,
sixty years later, 'He is—he is with Shakespeare.'

From *John Keats: The Making of a Poet*, The Viking Press, Inc.,
New York, 1963, pp. 414-15. Nine lines of the original and one
footnote have been omitted. Title supplied by the editor.

---

*... you perhaps at one time thought there was such a thing as Worldly
Happiness to be arrived at, at certain periods of time marked out—you
have of necessity from your disposition been thus led away—I
scarcely remember counting upon any Happiness—I look not for it
if it be not in the present hour—nothing startles me beyond the
Moment. The setting sun will always set me to rights—or if a Sparrow
come before my Window I take part in its existence and pick about
the Gravel. The first thing that strikes me on hea[r]ing a Misfortune
having befallen another is this. 'Well it cannot be helped.—he will
have the pleasure of trying the resourses of his spirit, and I beg now
my dear Bailey that hereafter should you observe any thing cold in
me not to but [for put] it to the account of heartlessness but abstraction—for I assure you I sometimes feel not the influence of a Passion
or Affection during a whole week—and so long this sometimes con-
tinues I begin to suspect myself and the genuiness of my feelings at
other times—thinking them a few barren Tragedy-tears ...*
(John Keats to Benjamin Bailey, November 22, 1817)

The Poet as Hero: Keats in His Letters

IN the history of literature the letters of John Keats are unique. All personal letters are interesting; the letters of great men naturally have an especial attraction; and among the letters of great men those of the great creative artists are likely to be the most intimate, the liveliest, and the fullest of wisdom. Yet even among the great artists Keats is perhaps the only one whose letters have an interest which is virtually equal to that of their writer's canon of created work. . . . because of the letters it is impossible to think of Keats only as a poet—inevitably we think of him as something even more interesting than a poet, we think of him as a man, and as a certain kind of man, a hero. . . .

The charm of Keats's letters is inexhaustible, and we can scarcely hope to define it wholly or to name all its elements. Yet we can be sure that some part of its effect comes from Keats's conscious desire to live life in the heroic mode. In a young man this is always most winning. Keats was situated in a small way of life, that of the respectable, liberal, intellectual middle part of the middle class; his field of action was limited to the small continuous duties of the family; his deportment was marked by quietness and modesty, at times by a sort of diffident neutrality. He nevertheless at every moment took life in the largest possible way and seems never to have been without the sense that to be, or to become, a man was an adventurous problem. The phrase in his letters that everyone knows, 'life is a vale of soul-making', is his summing up of that sense, which, once we have become aware of its existence in him, we understand to have dominated his mind. He believed that life was given for him to find the right use of it, that it was a kind of continuous magical confrontation requiring to be met with the right answer. He believed that this answer was to be derived from intuition, courage, and the accumulation of experience. It was not, of course, to be a formula of any kind, not a piece of rationality, but rather a way of being and of acting. And yet it could in part be derived from taking thought, and it could be put, if not into a formula, then at least into many formulations. Keats was nothing if not a man of ideas.

His way of conceiving of life is characteristic of the spirited young man of high gifts—except that it is also characteristic of the very great older men whom the young men of spirit and gifts are most likely to take seriously. Its charm in Keats is the greater because its span is so short and so dramatically concise. Keats is twenty when the letters begin, and he is twenty-six when they end. But he was strikingly precocious—I am inclined to think even more precocious in his knowledge of the world than in poetry. He was one of that class of geniuses who early learn to trust themselves in an essential way, whatever moments of doubt they may have. He was remarkably lucky, or wise, in finding a circle of friends who believed in his powers before he had given much evidence of their existence beyond the communicated sense of his heroic vision, and these friends expected him to speak out. He therefore at a very early age passed beyond all self-conscious hesitation about looking deep into life and himself, about propounding the great questions and attempting the great answers, and about freely telling his thoughts. And so we have the first of the vital contradictions which make the fascination of Keats's mind—we have the wisdom of maturity arising from the preoccupations of youth. This wisdom is the proud, bitter, and joyful acceptance of tragic life which we associate pre-eminently with Shakespeare. It explains the force, as the sense of adventure explains the charm, of Keats's letters. . . .

THE PLEASURES OF THE SENSES

We cannot understand Keats's mind without a very full awareness of what powers of enjoyment he had and of how freely he licensed these powers. The pleasure of the senses was for him not merely desirable —it was the very ground of life. It was, moreover, the ground of thought. More than any other poet—more, really, than Shelley— Keats is Platonic, but his Platonism is not doctrinal or systematic: it was by the natural impulse of his temperament that his mind moved up the ladder of love which Plato expounds in *The Symposium*, beginning with the love of things and moving toward the love of ideas, with existences and moving toward essences, with appetites and moving toward immortal longings. But the movement is of a special kind, perhaps of a kind that the orthodox interpretation of Plato cannot approve. For it is not, so to speak, a biographical movement—Keats does not, as he develops, 'advance' from a preoccupation with sense to a preoccupation with intellect. Rather it is his characteristic mode of thought all through his life to begin with sense and to move thence to what he calls 'abstraction', but never to leave sense behind. Sense cannot be left behind, for of itself it generates the idea and remains continuous with it. And the moral and speculative intensity with which Keats's poems and letters are charged has its unique grace and illumination because it goes along with, and grows out of, and conditions, but does not deny, the full autonomy of sense.

But it is not enough to speak of Keats's loyalty to sense, nor is it even enough to speak of his loyalty to the pleasure of the senses. . . . Our language distinguishes between the sensory, the sensuous, and the sensual. The first word is neutral as regards pleasure, the second connotes pleasure of varying degrees and kinds but is yet distinguished from the last, which suggests pleasure that is intense, appetitive, material, and which usually carries a strong pejorative overtone and almost always an implication of sexuality. For Wordsworth the pleasures of the senses are the clear sign of rightness of life, but virtually the only two sense-faculties of which he takes account are seeing and hearing, and, at that, the seeing and hearing of only a few kinds of things; and the matter of the senses' experience passes very quickly into what Wordsworth calls the 'purer mind' and has been but minimally sensuous, let alone sensual. For Keats, however, there was no distinction of prestige among the senses, and to him the sensory, the sensuous, and the sensual were all one. . . . Wordsworth would have withdrawn hastily when Keats urges the newly married Reynolds to 'gorge the honey of life'. Particularly because of the sexual context, but not because of that alone, he would have been dismayed by the appetitive image and the frankness of appetite amounting to greed.

But it is, of course, exactly the appetitive image and the frankness of his appetite that we cannot dispense with in our understanding of Keats. Eating and the delicacies of taste are basic and definitive in his experience and in his poetry. The story of his putting cayenne pepper on his tongue in order to feel the more intensely the pleasure of a draft of cold claret is apocryphal. Yet it is significant that Haydon, who told the story, was sufficiently aware of Keats's disposition to have invented it. It does not, after all, go beyond Keats's own account of his pleasure in the nectarine. 'Talking of pleasure,' he writes to Dilke, 'this moment I was writing with one hand, and with the other holding to my mouth a Nectarine—good God how fine. It went down soft, slushy, oozy—all its delicious embonpoint melted down my throat like a beatified Strawberry.'

We are ambivalent in our conception of the moral status of eating and drinking. On the one hand ingestion supplies the imagery of our largest and most intense experiences: we speak of the wine of life and the cup of life; we speak also of its dregs and lees, and sorrow is also something to be drunk from a cup; shame and defeat are wormwood and gall; divine providence is manna or milk and honey; we hunger and thirst for righteousness; we starve for love; lovers devour each other with their eyes; and scarcely a mother has not exclaimed that oh, she could eat her baby up; bread and salt are the symbols of peace and loyalty, bread and wine the stuff of the most solemn acts of religion. On the other hand, however, while we may represent all of significant life by the tropes of eating and drinking, we do so with great circumspection. Our use of the ingestive imagery is rapid and sparse, never developed; we feel it unbecoming to dwell upon what we permit ourselves to refer to . . .

But with Keats the ingestive imagery is pervasive and extreme. He is possibly unique among poets in the extensiveness of his reference to eating and drinking and to its pleasurable or distasteful sensations. To some readers this is likely to be alienating, and indeed even a staunch admirer might well become restive under, for example, Keats's excessive reliance on the word 'dainties' to suggest all pleasures, even the pleasures of literature. . . . The ingestive appetite is the most primitive of our appetites, the sole appetite of our infant state, and a preoccupation with it, an excessive emphasis upon it, is felt— and not without some reason—to imply the passivity and self-reference of the infantile condition. . . .

But Keats . . . did not repress the infantile wish; he confronted it, recognized it, and delighted in it. Food—and what for the infant usually goes with food, a cozy warmth—made for him the form, the elementary idea, of felicity. He did not fear the seduction of the wish for felicity, because, it would seem, he was assured that the tendency of his being was not that of regression but that of growth. The knowledge of felicity was his first experience—he made it the ground of all experience, the foundation of his quest for truth. Thus, for Keats, the luxury of food is connected with, and in a sense gives place to, the luxury of sexuality. The best known example of this is the table spread with 'dainties' beside Madeline's bed in *The Eve of St Agnes*. And in that famous scene the whole paraphernalia of luxurious felicity, the invoked warmth of the south, the bland and delicate food, the privacy of the bed, and the voluptuousness of the sexual encounter, are made to glow into an island of bliss with the ultimate dramatic purpose of making fully apparent the cold surrounding darkness; it is the moment of life in the infinitude of not-being. As an image of man's life it has the force of the Venerable Bede's apologue of the sparrow that flew out of the night of winter storm through the warmth and light of the king's ale-hall and out again into darkness. Keats's capacity for pleasure implies his capacity for the apprehension of tragic reality.

It also serves his capacity for what he called *abstraction*. I have said that he was the most Platonic of poets. Ideas, abstractions, were his life. He lived to perceive ultimate things, essences. This is what appetite, or love, was always coming to mean for him. Plato said that Love is the child of Abundance and Want, and for Keats it was just that. In one of the most remarkable passages of his letters he says that the heart 'is the teat from which the mind or intelligence sucks identity'. The first appetite prefigures the last; the first ingestive image is constant for this man who, in his last sonnet, speaks of 'the palate of my mind', and who images the totality of life by the single grape which is burst against 'the palate fine'. . . .

NEGATIVE CAPABILITY AND THE PROBLEM OF EVIL

When Keats concludes his remarks about Negative Capability with the observation that 'with a great poet the sense of Beauty overcomes every other consideration, or rather obliterates all consideration', meaning all considerations of what is disagreeable or painful, it may seem that he has evaded the issue, that, having raised the question of painful truth in art, he betrays it to beauty in a statement that really has no meaning. It is in this way that many readers understand the concluding aphorism, the 'moral', of the *Ode to a Grecian Urn*—out of politeness to poetry they may consent to be teased, but they cannot suppose that they are enlightened by the statement, 'Beauty is truth, truth beauty', for, as they say, beauty is not all of truth, and not all truth is beautiful. Nor will they be the more disposed to find meaning in the notorious aphorism by the poet's extravagant assertion that in it is to be found 'all/Ye know on earth, and all ye need to know'.

But the statement, 'Beauty is truth, truth beauty', was not for Keats, and need not be for us, a 'pseudo-statement', large, resonant, engaging, but without actual significance. Beauty was not for Keats, as it is for many, an inert thing, or a thing whose value lay in having no relevance to ordinary life: it was not a word by which he evaded, but a word by which he confronted, issues. What he is saying in his letter is that a great poet, (e.g. Shakespeare) looks at human life, sees the terrible truth of its evil, but sees it so intensely that it becomes an element of the beauty which is created by his act of perception—in the phrase by which Keats describes his own experience as merely a reader of *King Lear,* he 'burns through' the evil. To say, as many do, that 'truth is beauty' is a false statement is to ignore our experience of the tragic art. Keats's statement is an accurate description of the response to evil or ugliness which tragedy makes: the matter of tragedy is ugly or painful truth seen as beauty. To see life in this way, Keats believes, is to see life truly: that is, as it must be seen if we are to endure to live it. Beauty is thus a middle term which connects and reconciles two kinds of truth—through the mediation of beauty, truth of fact becomes truth of affirmation, truth of life. . . .

This way of seeing life, the poet's way, characterized by 'intensity', is obviously anything but a 'negative' capability—it is the most *positive* capability imaginable. But Keats understood it to be protected and made possible by Negative Capability: the poet avoids making those doctrinal utterances about the nature of life, about life's goodness or badness or perfectibility, which, if he rests in them, will prevent his going on to his full poetic vision. . . . It is not all of truth that Keats is concerned with but rather that truth which is to be discovered between the contradiction of love and death, between the sense of personal identity and the certainty of pain and extinction. . . .

The problem of evil lies at the very heart of Keats's thought. But for Keats the awareness of evil exists side by side with a very strong sense of personal identity . . .

Now Keats's attachment to the principle of reality was, as I have said, a strong one. He perceived the fact of evil very clearly, and he put it at the very centre of his mental life. He saw, as he said, 'too far into the sea' and beheld there the 'eternal fierce destruction' of the struggle for existence, and the shark and the hawk at prey taught him that the gentle and habitual robin was not less predatory, that life in its totality was cruel; he saw youth grow pale and spectre-thin and die, saw life trod down by life, the hungry generations on the march. For all his partisanship with social amelioration, he had no hope whatever that life could be ordered in such a way that its condition might be anything but tragic. . . .

But at the same time that Keats had his clear knowledge of evil, he had his equally clear knowledge of the self. Most of us are conventional in our notions of reality and we suppose that what is grim and cruel is more real than what is pleasant. Like most conventionalities of thought, this one is a form of power-worship—evil and pain seem realer to us than the assertions of the self because we know that evil and pain always win in the end. But Keats did not share in our acquiescence. His attachment to reality was stronger and more complex than ours usually is, for to him the self was just as real as the evil that destroys it. The idea of reality and the idea of the self and its annihilation go together for him. 'After all there is certainly something real in the World—. . . . Tom [his brother] has spit a leetle blood this afternoon, and that is rather a damper—but I know—the truth is there is something real in the World.' He conceives of the energy of the self as at least one source of reality. 'As Tradesmen say every thing is worth what it will fetch, so probably every mental pursuit takes its reality and worth from the ardour of the pursuer—being in itself a nothing.' And again: 'I am certain of nothing but of the holiness of the heart's affections and the truth of the Imagination— What the Imagination seizes as Beauty must be truth—whether it

existed before or not—for I have the same Idea of all our Passions as
of Love they are all, in their sublime, creative of essential Beauty. . . .
The Imagination may be compared to Adam's dream [in *Paradise Lost*]
—he awoke and found it truth.'
He affirms, that is, the creativity of the self that opposes circumstance, the self that is imagination and desire, that, like Adam, assigns
names and values to things, and that can realize what it envisions.

Keats never deceives himself into believing that the power of the
imagination is sovereign, that it can make the power of circumstance
of no account. His sense of the stubborn actuality of the material
world is as stalwart as Wordsworth's. It is, indeed, of the very nature
of his whole intellectual and moral activity that he should hold in
balance the reality of self and the reality of circumstance. In another
letter to Bailey he makes the two realities confront each other in a
very telling way. He is speaking of the malignity of society toward
generous enthusiasm and, as he goes on, his thought moves from the
life of society to touch upon the cosmos, whose cruelty, as he thinks
of it, impels him to reject the life in poetry and the reward of fame
he so dearly wants. 'Were it in my choice,' he says, 'I would reject a
petrarchal coronation—on account of my dying day and because
women have cancers.' But then in the next sentence but one: 'And
yet I am not old enough or magnanimous enough to annihilate self. . . .'
He has brought his two knowledges face to face, the knowledge of the
world of circumstance, of death and cancer, and the knowledge of the
world of self, of spirit and creation, and the delight in them. Each
seems a whole knowledge considered alone; each is but a half-
knowledge when taken with the other; both together constitute a truth.

It is in terms of the self confronting hostile or painful circumstance
that Keats makes his magnificent effort at the solution of the problem
of evil, his heroic attempt to show how it is that life may be called
blessed when its circumstances are cursed. This occurs in the course
of his dazzling letter to George and Georgiana Keats in Kentucky
which he began on February 14, 1819, and sealed on May 3rd. It is a
massive journal-letter into which Keats copies, among lesser examples
of his work, the sonnet *Why did I laugh to-night?, the two sonnets*
on fame, *La Belle Dame Sans Merci*, the sonnet on sleep and the
sonnet on rhyme, and the *Ode to Psyche*. It is crammed full of gossip,
personal, literary, and theatrical, and equally full of Keats's most serious
and characteristic thought. The letter, indeed, is the quintessence of
Keats's life-style, of his way of dealing with experience. It is one of
the most remarkable documents of the culture of the century.

The climax of the letter occurs in the last full entry, that of April
15th, in which Keats makes his dead-set at the problem of evil. This
entry is the first after that of March 19th, which in itself constitutes a

very notable episode in Keats's intellectual life. The earlier entry is Keats's attempt to deal with the problem in aesthetic terms, as the later is his attempt to deal with it in moral terms. In the March 19th entry he writes that he is in a state of languorous relaxation in which 'pleasure has no show of enticement and pain no unbearable frown', a condition which he calls 'the only happiness'. But at the moment of setting this down he receives a note from Haslam telling of the imminently expected death of his friend's father, and he is led to speak of the ironic mutability of life. 'While we are laughing the seed of some trouble is put into the wide arable land of event—while we are laughing it sprouts it grows and suddenly bears a poison fruit which we must pluck.' Then follows a meditation on our inability really to respond to the troubles of our friends and on the virtue of 'disinterestedness'. This leads to the thought that disinterestedness, so great a virtue in society, is not to be found in 'wild nature', where its presence, indeed, would destroy the natural economy of tooth and claw. But from the spectacle of self-interested cruelty of wild nature he snatches the idea of the brilliance of the energies that are in play in the struggle for existence. 'This is what makes the Amusement of Life—to a speculative Mind. I go among the Fields and catch a glimpse of a Stoat or a fieldmouse peeping out of the withered grass—the creature hath a purpose and its eyes are bright with it. I go among the buildings of a city and I see a Man hurrying along—to what? the creature hath a purpose and his eyes are bright with it.' He thinks of the disinterestedness of Jesus and of how little it has established itself as against the self-interest of men, and again he snatches at the idea that perhaps life may be justified by its sheer energy: 'May there not be superior beings amused by any graceful, though instinctive attitude my mind may fall into, as I am entertained with the alertness of a Stoat or the anxiety of a Deer? Though a quarrel in the Streets is a thing to be hated, the energies displayed in it are fine; the commonest Man shows a grace in his quarrel—By a superior being our reasonings may take the same tone—though erroneous they may be fine—This is the very thing in which consists poetry—'

It is very brilliant, very fine, but it does not satisfy him; 'amusement', 'entertainment' are not enough. Even poetry is not enough. Energy is the very thing 'in which consists poetry'—'and if so it is not so fine a thing as philosophy—For the same reason that an eagle is not so fine a thing as a truth.'

'Give me credit—' he cries across the broad Atlantic. 'Do you not think I strive—to know myself? Give me this credit—' We cannot well refuse it.

The simple affirmation of the self in its vital energy means much to him, but it does not mean enough, and in the time intervening between the entry of March 19th and that of April 15th his mind has been moving toward the reconciliation of energy and truth, of passion and principle. He has been reading, he says, Robertson's *America* and Voltaire's *Siècle de Louis XIV* and his mind is full of the miseries of man in either a simple or a highly civilized state. He canvasses the possibilities of amelioration of the human fate and concludes that our life even at its conceivable best can be nothing but tragic, the very elements and laws of nature being hostile to man. Then, having stated as extremely as this the case of human misery, he breaks out with sudden contempt for those who call the world a vale of tears. 'What a little circumscribed straightened notion!' he says. 'Call the world if you please "The vale of Soul-making!" . . . I say "*Soul making*"—Soul as distinguished from an Intelligence—There may be intelligences or sparks of the divinity in millions—but they are not Souls till they acquire identities, till each one is personally itself.'

There follows a remarkable flight into a sort of transcendental psychology in the effort to suggest how intelligences become souls, and then: 'Do you not see how necessary a World of Pains and troubles is to school an Intelligence and make it a Soul? A Place where the heart must feel and suffer in a thousand different ways'. And the heart is 'the teat from which the Mind or intelligence sucks its identity'.

He writes with an animus against Christian doctrine, but what he is giving, he says, is a sketch of *salvation*. . . .

The faculty of Negative Capability has yielded doctrine—for the idea of soul-making, of souls creating themselves in their confrontation of circumstance, is available to Keats's conception only because he has remained with half-knowledge, with the double knowledge of the self and of the world's evil.

From the Introduction to *The Selected Letters of John Keats*, Edited by Lionel Trilling, Farrar, Straus & Young, New York, 1951, pp. 3–41. The essay has been abridged. Subtitles supplied by the editor.

. . . We hate poetry that has a palpable design upon us—and if we do not agree, seems to put its hand in its breeches pocket. Poetry should be great & unobtrusive, a thing which enters into one's soul, and does not startle it or amaze it with itself but with its subject.—How beautiful are the retired flowers! how would they lose their beauty were they to throng into the highway crying out, 'admire me I am a violet! dote upon me I am a primrose! . . .

(John Keats to J. H. Reynolds, February 3, 1818)

E. C. PETTET

Keats's Romanticism

THERE are three poets who have been unaffected by the sharp depreciation of the Romantic period in twentieth-century criticism—Blake, Wordsworth, and, with some exceptions, Keats. The reputations of Blake and Wordsworth, both essential Romantics, have survived (and indeed increased) probably because we feel that these two poets express much of what is most significant and permanently valuable in the Romantic revolution. Keats, on the other hand, has been protected by a process of isolation. . . . We have been encouraged to think of him as transcending his age much as the immeasurably greater genius of Shakespeare transcends the Elizabethan period. Middleton Murry's influential study represents a notable instance of this isolating kind of critical approach, and certainly a very strong case can be made for regarding Keats as the least romantic of the great Romantic poets.

Complex and baffling as Romanticism is to define, there can be little doubt that the heart of it . . . was what Keats in some observation on the poetical character once described as the 'egotistical sublime'— the cult of original, distinctive personality, the impassioned belief in individualism, the use of poetry primarily for self-projection, self-analysis, self-assertion, and ultimately sometimes for exhibitionism and self-gratification. The first and foremost article of the Romantic creed was the affirmation of a god-like 'I' that makes the poetic world and that, in creating poetry, creates itself.

Keats not only dissented from this article but consciously and consistently maintained an antithetical belief. Against poetry of the 'Wordsworthian or egotistical sublime', introverted writing that draws all experience into the poet's ego and insists on shaping it to those subjective attitudes and beliefs that constitute 'character', Keats upheld the ideal of a selfless, unrestricted, outflowing sensibility—a poetry of which drama is the highest form. . . .

On the whole Keats's poetry conforms to the ideas about the poetic character that he expresses in his letters. For one thing we notice that, unlike some of the Romantic poets, he devoted only a small part of his energies to the chief poetic form of subjective writing. The inevitable prominence of the odes easily leads us to overlook the fact that lyric poetry is often a quite minor by-product of his activities, and indeed even the odes were regarded by himself as incidental work. The lyrical poems he did write are never the compositions of a 'large self-worshipper', and many of them (including, with one or two exceptions, the best) are mainly of an impersonal kind. We cannot read them, like the lyrics of Byron and Shelley, as fragments of a continual spiritual autobiography. Certainly there is some deeply felt personal experience behind the odes of 1819; but the significant fact is that this experience is *behind* the odes, not their substance, and that the poetic 'I' is to a large extent a universalized one. This is the chief measure of difference between, say, the *Ode to a Nightingale* and *Dejection: an Ode*; between the ode *To Autumn* and the *Ode to the West Wind*. Further, when we read some of the most personal of Keats's lyrics (the ode *To Fanny*, 'The day is gone', 'I cry your mercy', for instance), we feel that while these poems are thoroughly Romantic they are only momentarily, and not typically, Keatsian. And sometimes, as notably in the 'Bright star' sonnet, there is a curious blend of objective writing and romantic confessional outpouring in the same lyric.

Similar observations hold good for Keats's longer poems, which, constituting the main part of his work, were regarded by him as steps towards his ambition in the most objective form of poetry, poetic drama. Some of these poems can be related to his personal experience, and he undoubtedly entertained a growing belief that his poetry should be expressive of his own deepest preoccupations. For all this, there is very little of the obsessions, of the projection and self-dramatization, the masks and thinly disguised autobiography, that we find in the longer poems of Byron and Shelley. Even in *Lamia,* though it is extremely tempting to interpret the Lycius-Lamia-Apollonius triangle in terms of Keats, Fanny Brawne and Charles Brown, we cannot be really sure that this is the right way to read the poem; if there is autobiography, it is certainly related with an un-Romantic obliqueness.

Closely involved in the egocentricity of Romanticism there was its non-conformity, its Prometheanism (or Satanism) that ranged from a spirit of vague unrest to loud defiance and revolt. With one exception ... there is nothing of this attitude in Keats's poetry. He was interested in politics and stood on the left of his time; when in 1819 it seemed that he would have to turn to journalism for a living, he was insistent that his writing should be 'on the liberal side of the question'. But for all Bernard Shaw's approval of the description of the capitalist exploitations of Lorenzo's employers (*Isabella,* stanzas XIV–XVII), this strong liberalism of Keats had little effect on his poetry and none that seriously matters. So, too, in religion. The letters leave the impression of a free-thinking agnostic; but Keats was no atheist or Romantic diabolist, and we find him seriously—and informatively—advising his sister on her confirmation.... In any event, whatever Keats's private doubts about immortality, the divinity of Christ, or other parts of the Christian faith, he never used his poetry for the expression of free-thinking speculations.

Yet another of Keats's striking departures from the central creed of Romanticism is indicated by his remark, 'Scenery is fine—but human nature is finer.'

Though this opinion, which sounds so much more Augustan than Romantic, is repeated several times in the letters, in remarks like 'I am getting a great dislike of the picturesque', some readers may find it hard to believe that Keats really meant what he said, for it is a persisting effect of the Romantic Revolution that many of us are inclined to think of 'Nature' as an essential constituent of poetry. Yet Keats's remark has a true bearing on his poetic work, since while nature furnishes a large part of his imagery (though much less from *Hyperion* onwards), it rarely provided the direct and powerful inspiration that Wordsworth and Shelley experienced, and he wrote few poems that consisted primarily of natural description. Again, in spite of his long expedition into the Lake District and Scotland and his journey home by sea, he had singularly little of the Romantic taste for the wild and awe-inspiring manifestations of nature, for mountains, wastes, seas, storm and tempests.... What Keats enjoyed in nature he enjoyed with a simple, intense sensuousness; and Wordsworth's well-known comment on his 'paganism', tactless and ungracious as it was for the occasion, was not so very wide of the mark. There is nothing in his poetry of the common Romantic tendency to identify scenes and landscapes with subjective moods and emotions; nothing of the contagious Wordsworthian conviction of some spiritual significance in nature; and indeed—one or two possibly controversial passages of *Endymion* apart—no sense of mystery at all.... In spite of his fluency of expression, and in spite of his confession that the *Ode to Psyche* was the only poem 'with which I have taken even moderate pains. I have for the most part dash'd off my lines in a hurry', there is abundant MS evidence to show that he often laboured hard to achieve perfect expression. One small but interesting example of this habit of working over the initial inspiration is furnished by those endlessly quoted lines in the *Ode to a Nightingale*—

> Charm'd magic casements, opening on the foam
> Of perilous seas, in faery lands forlorn.

These lines have frequently been instanced as pure and purely spontaneous poetry, in which every word is compulsively inevitable. Per-

haps that is our final impression, but it is something of a shock to see
for the first time the autograph in the Fitzwilliam Museum, Cambridge (especially if M. R. Ridley is right in his belief that there was an
earlier rough draft to this autograph) and to notice how the felicity of
these lines has emerged through the alterations of

> Charm'd the wide casements, opening on the foam
> Of ruthless [or, keeless?] seas, in fairy lands forlorn.

Such alert and patient reconsideration of lines, along with the
numerous acute observations on the art of poetry that are scattered
through his letters, certainly justifies Garrod's contention that 'more
than most of our poets Keats was truly a student of his art'. It is this
characteristic that distinguishes him from most of the Romantic poets,
especially from those of his own generation, for if they occasionally
philosophized generally about poetry, by and large they did not think
much about its technique, nor, rating inspiration and rapture so highly,
were they fond of the arduous labour of revision. They wrote most
commonly on a 'hit or miss' principle, trusting that the mysterious
power of poetic inspiration would ensure more hits than misses and
reluctant to tamper with the products of that inspiration. Keats stands
apart from them as an 'artist' who, though he may have underesti-
mated Shelley's purely poetic qualities, had every right to advise his
great contemporary to 'be more of an artist'.

However, while Keats's work contains much that is remote from the
main body of Romantic poetry, it also belongs to its historical time
and place. For all the large exceptions we must make, Keats *is* an
English Romantic poet, and if we ignore this fact we are always in
danger of lapsing into unsound and even unsympathetic criticism. This
danger, as the writing of Middleton Murry often shows, is particularly
insidious when we discuss Romantic features of Keats's poetry without
realizing that they are Romantic.

We have recently suggested that Keats's sense of poetic craftsmanship, his consciousness of himself as an 'artist', is exceptional for his
time. On the other hand, we must understand that his attitude to his
art was also in several important respects a thoroughly Romantic
one. . . . For most of his life he wrote out of an assured Romantic
belief in the transcendent value of poetry; and the Induction to *The
Fall of Hyperion* is a decisive testament to this belief. Facing up to his
most searching doubts, believing and accepting that in a world of so
much misery the true poet is doomed to an exceptional burden of pain,
he unswervingly re-affirmed his conviction that poetry—if not of the
kind that he had mainly written, at least the poetry he would one day
write—is supremely worthwhile.

With this Romantic belief in the supreme value of poetry he dedicated himself to it, absolutely. Nothing else really mattered. 'I find that I cannot exist without poetry—without eternal poetry—half the day will not do—the whole of it—I began with a little, but habit has made me a Leviathan.'...In one very important sense he is a Romantic egotist, notwithstanding his completely sincere rejection of poetry of the 'egotistical sublime'. Measure him by his most deeply considered and responsible statement on the nature of poetry, the Induction to *The Fall of Hyperion,* and we discover that all his preoccupation is with what poetry means to him, with poetry as the mode of his own spiritual development.... *The Fall of Hyperion* is the revolutionary Romantic claim that the poet creates primarily to create himself. Elsewhere he makes the claim quite consciously and explicitly, as when he confesses, 'I never wrote one single Line of Poetry with the least Shadow of public thought'....

There may be some doubt about the significance of these attitudes for Keats's poetry; there can be none about his belief in the supreme value of the imagination, which, perhaps more than anything else, stamps him as a poet of the Romantic movement. At the centre of his first important poem of any length, *Sleep and Poetry,* there is the question:

> Is there so small a range
> In the present strength of manhood, that the high
> Imagination cannot freely fly
> As she was wont of old?

and in this manifesto poem, castigating eighteenth-century verse mainly for its lack of imaginative qualities. Keats dedicates himself to the revival of imagination in English poetry. Again, towards the end of his short poetic life, in September 1819, we find him making this critical distinction between Byron and himself: 'There is this great difference between us. He describes what he sees—I describe what I imagine.'...

Again, in our twentieth-century criticism we have heard a great deal about Keats's concept of imagination as a power, closely associated with sensation, intuition, and visionary insight, by which we may apprehend (and, if poets, create) a certain kind of philosophic 'truth' that is correlative with 'beauty'—'What the imagination seizes as Beauty must be truth— whether it existed before or not.' Admittedly this idea of imagination is echoed, as idea, in several of the poems; but apart from the Induction to *The Fall of Hyperion,* possibly *Hyperion* itself, and possibly (but by no means certainly) one or two of the odes, Keats's poetic work as a whole cannot be regarded as the expression of a significant body of truth that has been apprehended, or created, by the poetic imagination. In the reaction against the nineteenth-century idea of Keats as a poet merely of the senses, a worshipper of beauty, there has been far too much legerdemain between brilliant speculative passages in his letters and the poems he actually wrote. . . .

The 'imagination' of which Keats's poems are truly the fruit takes two main forms. In the first place the world of his poetry—of the long and narrative poems in particular—is predominantly an artificial one, or, to use the word in its familiar sense from his differentiation between Byron and himself, one that he *imagines* rather than reflects from direct experience. Further, in this simpler sense of 'imagining', he has all the Romantic fondness for the unfamiliar and strange and for the remote in place and time. One of the most obvious manifestations of this is his medievalism: it was an intoxicating draught from *The Faerie Queene* that first turned him into a poet, and from the *Calidore* verses to the *Eve of St Agnes* and *La Belle Dame Sans Merci* his work is filled with attempts to express the

> shadows haunting fairily
> The brain, new stuff'd, in youth, with triumphs gay
> Of old romance.

No less pronounced, from *Endymion* to the *Ode on a Grecian Urn* and *Lamia,* was his attempt to body forth a dream of the Grecian world and its mythology,

> Of deities or mortals, or of both,
> In Tempe or the dales of Arcady;

and this combination of classical and medieval dream in his poetry makes it unique among the work of the English Romantics, who usually confine themselves to one or the other. In the second place, Keats's poetry is of the imagination in the sense that a great deal of it, even of the odes, is a vision of what he would like human life to be—an expression of desires, longings, and aspirations stimulated by, and as time went on more and more in conflict with, his own experience of pain and misery. This does not mean . . . that his work is filled with direct confessional outpourings in the common Romantic manner. Almost always his dreaming is objectified or universalized; and we can appreciate this important distinction if we compare his *Eve of St Agnes,* a day-dream of happy, fulfilled love, with Shelley's love-poem *Epipsychidion.* In the *Eve of St Agnes* Keats is speaking for all of us in love; in *Epipsychidion* Shelley is speaking (and dreaming) chiefly for his own highly individual self. . . .

Finally, to round off this short account of the Romantic in Keats, we may briefly note several other features: . . . the abundance of imagery drawn from nature, the recurrent theme of destructive love and the Fatal Woman, the continued note of 'joy of grief', and the deep obsession with sleep, dreams, and death.

From *On The Poetry of John Keats*, CUP, Cambridge, 1957, pp. 282–98. The chapter has been abridged and footnotes have been omitted.

. . . It has been an old Comparison for our urging on—the Bee hive— however it seems to me that we should rather be the flower than the Bee—for it is a false notion that more is gained by receiving than giving—no the receiver and the giver are equal in their benefits— The f[l]ower I doubt not receives a fair guerdon from the Bee—its leaves blush deeper in the next spring—and who shall say between Man and Woman which is the most delighted? Now it is more noble to sit like Jove that [for than] to fly like Mercury—let us not there- fore go hurrying about and collecting honey-bee like, buzzing here and there impatiently from a knowledge of what is to be arrived at: but let us open our leaves like a flower and be passive and receptive— budding patiently under the eye of Apollo and taking hints from evey noble insect that favors us with a visit—sap will be given us for Meat and dew for drink—I was led into these thoughts, my dear Reynolds, by the beauty of the morning operating on a sense of Idleness—I have not read any Books—the Morning said I was right—I had no Idea but of the Morning and the Thrush said I was right— . . .

(John Keats to J. H. Reynolds, February 19, 1818)

. . . In Poetry I have a few Axioms, and you will see how far I am from their Centre. 1st I think Poetry should surprise by a fine excess and not by Singularity—it should strike the Reader as a wording of his own highest thoughts, and appear almost a Remembrance—2nd Its touches of Beauty should never be half way therby making the reader breathless instead of content: the rise, the progress, the setting of imagery should like the Sun come natural too him—shine over him and set soberly although in magnificence leaving him in the Luxury of twilight—but it is easier to think what Poetry should be than to write it—and this leads me on to another axiom. That if Poetry comes not as naturally as the Leaves to a tree it had better not come at all. . . .

(John Keats to John Taylor, February 27, 1818)

W. JACKSON BATE

Keats's Style: Evolution Toward Qualities of Permanent Value

IT is during the year or more following the writing of *Isabella* that the maturer style of Keats developed so rapidly. Among the primary characteristics of this style is a suggestive power of image capable of securing from the reader an unusually intense emotional and imaginative identification. This quality has become widely recognized in recent years, particularly since the implications of Keats's own conception of the poet's character, and of his puzzling term, 'Negative Capability', have been discussed. We need not here make distinctions between the romantic theory of sympathetic identification, in which the poet takes on, through participation, the qualities and character of his object, and the more recent theory of *Einfühlung* (or empathy), with its suggestion that many of these qualities are merely the subjective creation of the poet or observer, and are bestowed upon the object rather than descried in it. The poetry of Keats contains abundant examples that might be used to substantiate either, or both at once, as a guiding characteristic of his verse.

Certainly, in the verse written before *Hyperion,* a subjective element—more empathic than sympathetic—often characterizes this imaginative identification ('sweet peas, on *tiptoe* for a flight', the foam crawling along the back of the wave with a 'wayward indolence'). But a more sympathetic in-feeling is equally apparent (minnows 'staying their wavy bodies 'gainst the stream', lions with 'nervy tails', or the organic in-feeling in 'Ere a lean bat could plump its wintry skin'). The verse from *Hyperion* through the great odes is replete with such imagery, ranging from 'The hare *limp'd trembling* through the frozen grass' to the agonies of the huge figures in *Hyperion*: 'horrors, portion'd to a giant nerve,/Oft made Hyperion ache'; or

> through all his bulk an agony
> Crept gradual, from the feet unto the crown,

> Like a lithe serpent vast and muscular,
> Making slow way, with head and neck convuls'd
> From over strainèd might . . .

                                             (I. 259–63)

Such lines remind us of the passages in both Shakespeare and Milton that evoked so strong a sympathetic participation in Keats—as, for example, when he wrote in the margin beside *Paradise Lost*, IX, 179 ff., where Satan enters the serpent without arousing him from sleep:

'Satan having entered the Serpent, and inform'd his brutal sense— might seem sufficient—but Milton goes on *but his sleep disturbed not*. Whose spirit does not ache at the smothering and confinement . . . the *waiting close?* Whose head is not dizzy at the possible speculations of Satan in the serpent prison? No passage of poetry ever can give a greater pain of suffocation.'

Or again there is his enthusiastic mention, in one of his letters (November 22, 1817), of Shakespeare's image of the sensitive retreat of a snail:

> As the snail, whose tender horns being hit,
> Shrinks back into his shelly cave with pain.

And we may recall Charles Cowden Clarke's story of Keats's reaction, while reading the *Faerie Queene* as a boy, to the phrase, 'sea-shouldering whales': as if raising himself against the pressure of the waves, 'he hoisted himself up, and looked burly and dominant. . . .'

This kinaesthetic gift of image, if one wishes to call it that, this organically felt participation, is further revealed in Keats's ability to bring into focus several diverse sense-impressions of an object, and —in transmuting them into a single image or series of images—present a more valid, rounded, and fully realized apperception. This unifying interplay of sense-impressions should not be confused with synaesthesia. Keats's imagery, to be sure, is perhaps as richly packed with examples of suggestive synaesthesia as any that can be found ('*fragrant* and enwreathèd light', 'pale and silver silence', 'scarlet pain', 'the *touch* of *scent*'), and Keats's use of it had more effect on the synaesthetic imagery of later English poetry than any other one model. But the really distinctive quality in Keats—and a quality his Victorian imitators rarely attained—is less the *substitution* than it is the *substantiation* of one sense by another in order to give, as it were, additional dimension and depth, as in 'the *moist scent* of flowers', 'embalmèd darkness', or in making incense tangibly 'soft' and visible:

> I cannot see what flowers are at my feet,
> Nor what soft incense hangs upon the boughs.

A further example is Keats's predilection for tactile qualities: his craving for touch ('Touch,' he wrote, 'has a memory'), and for a firm grasp of the concrete as it exists in space. Thus images directly or indirectly connected with the sense of taste are sustained and deepened, in their vitality, through associations with tactile and muscular response: the 'purple-stained mouth,' the nightingale singing of summer 'in *full-throated* ease,' or the closing stanza of the *Ode on Melancholy*, with its

> *aching* Pleasure nigh,
> Turning to poison while the *bee-mouth sips* . . .
> Though seen of none save him whose *strenuous tongue*
> Can *burst* Joy's *grape against his palate* fine. . . .

This tactile strength gives a three-dimensional grasp to Keats's images. Perhaps the most notable instance is the famous 'wealth of *globèd* peonies', in the same ode: here the hand is virtually enclosing the peony, further assuring itself of the three-dimensional roundness.

There is, in short, a *centring* in Keats's imagery of the various qualities of an object into a single apperception; and as a result the object emerges as a totality with its several aspects resolved into a unified whole rather than delineated or suggested separately. The use of strong tactile associations that give a firmer hold, a more definitely felt outline, is one means by which this centring of impressions, into an amalgamated whole, is secured and anchored. His general amassing and condensing of sense-impressions is another. And the result is an imagery that is less 'synaesthetic', in the ordinary sense, than it is a gifted illustration of what Hazlitt meant by 'gusto'—that is, a state in which the imagination, through sympathetic excitement, draws out and expresses the total character of its object. In this intense identification, the impressions made on one sense 'excite by affinity those of another'; the object is grasped as a vital whole. And accompanying this sympathetic gusto, with its resolving of diverse impressions into a unified and immediate experience, is a discerning ability to sense organic motion, with a vivid fellow-feeling, and as an unfolding and continuing process. One is reminded of Severn's account:

> 'a wave . . . billowing through a tree', as he described the uplifting surge of air among swaying masses of chestnuts or oak foliage, or when, afar off, he heard the wind coming across woodlands. 'The tide! the tide!' he would cry delightedly, and spring on to some stile, or upon the bough of a wayside tree, and watch the passage of the wind upon the meadow grasses or young corn, not stirring till the flow of air was all around him, while an expression of rapture made his eyes gleam and his face glow . . .

We can certainly note in [the] odes—especially the *Ode on a Grecian Urn* and the *Ode to a Nightingale*—what I can only call a successful intrusion of the dramatic. In each we are dealing with a miniature drama. In each the poet seeks at the start—in the *Ode to a Nightingale* shortly after the start—to identify himself with an object that can lift himself beyond a world of flux. In each there is a gradual disengagement, an inability to follow completely the implications of sympathetic absorption, and a return back (implicit in the *Grecian Urn,* more obvious in the *Nightingale*) to the world of process and the claims of the human heart. So, a century later with Yeats, there may be the paeans to Byzantium; but the drama lies in the return back—the descent down the ladder, as in 'The Circus Animals' Desertion'—to the human condition, and the assertive, unstilled desires of the dying animal, from which 'all ladders start'. The structure of the odes cannot be considered apart from this drama. Nor can the massive richness and the courageous openness to the full concrete expression, be considered apart from the drama, especially at a time like the present when fear of the welter, and quick unpredictable decay or change of concrete life has so intimidated the imagination of writers. There is courage here, in this welcome of concrete amplitude by Keats; and the courage is not apart from the poetic art.

The poems of the summer and early autumn of 1819 add important nuances to the situation. The questioning, before the odes, of the value and function of poetry in such a world as we find ourselves becomes more articulate in the letters. Energetic changes in style and form follow. *Lamia* drops, for the time being, many of the stylistic qualities of Keats from *Hyperion* through the odes. We have now a fairly open allegory, in some ways impetuously ironic and mocking in tone, which had, he hoped, a new energy that would 'take hold of people in some way—give them either pleasant or unpleasant sensations'. As if in a deliberate attempt to put things at arm's length, he surprisingly reverts to the crisp heroic couplet (the 'rocking-horse' metre he had once shied away from) of Dryden and Pope, though with a vivid colour all of his own. The couplet is not so closed as in Dryden or Pope; but there are many closer similarities of a minor prosodic nature. Whatever else may be said of *Lamia*, it treats the effect of a Circian enchantment upon the impressionable mind of a young man (Lycius) who is open to the appeal of a magic world, and who is unable to withstand reality when it is pointed out to him. This general theme is closely related to the style which Keats, within two months, has suddenly evolved in contrast to the odes.

But at the same time he has begun to disengage himself from this new style, and to turn to still another, though the fragmentary form of the *Fall of Hyperion*—the revised *Hyperion*—hardly shows it to advantage. For, leaving aside all the psychological difficulties of this impetuous period, he was dealing with a discarded fragment. Little can be said about the style of this recast and warmed-up fragment except about metre and idiom. Stripped of its original allegory, the poem indicts the 'dreamer' who makes poetry a means of escape from the concrete world. Keats strips the poem, too, of many of its Miltonic mannerisms. In the place of the grandeur of the first *Hyperion*, we have now a more mellow blank verse, Virgilian and half-pastoral in tone:

> Still was more plenty than the fabled horn
> Thrice emptied could pour forth, at banqueting
> For Proserpine return'd to her own fields,
> Where the white heifers low.

I, 35–38

> When in mid-May the sickening East Wind
> Shifts sudden to the South, the small warm rain
> Melts out the frozen incense from all flowers.

I, 97–99

Despite the uncertainty of the poem as a whole, there is a relaxed, even confident, quietness in the opening hundred lines or so of this revision. This opening can be said to suggest a style unlike anything else in the nineteenth century: a style towards which Keats might well have moved—or through which he would have passed to something else—had he continued to write for a few more years. Meanwhile, Keats's last great poem—the ode *To Autumn*—is, of course, a return to the full and dense richness that characterized the great odes of the preceding May, but a richness now harmonized and lifted to a serenity quite unequalled elsewhere in romantic poetry.

From *The Major English Romantic Poets: A symposium in Reappraisal*, Ed. Clarence D. Thorpe, Carlos Baker, Bennett Weaver, Southern Illinois University Press, Carbondale, 1957, pp. 217–30. This extract is taken from pp. 221–3 and 227–8 of the original essay.

...I have but lately stood on my guard against Milton. Life to him would be death to me.... The only means of strengthening one's intellect is to make up ones mind about nothing—to let the mind be a thoroughfare for all thoughts.
(John Keats to George and Georgiana Keats, September 24, 1819)

JOHN MIDDLETON MURRY

The Realms of Gold

KEATS'S sonnet *On First Looking into Chapman's Homer* holds a position of peculiar significance in his work as a whole: for several reasons: because it is one of the finest sonnets in the English language; because it is the first entirely successful poem that he wrote; because he wrote it very early in his poetic career—in the very month, October 1816, in which he became twenty-one, and decided, to his guardian's consternation, to abandon medicine for poetry; because it was to take him many months, even of his brief and crowded poetic life, to reach such assured mastery again; and finally because he wrote it very quickly. There are not many poems so well worth studying as this one. . . .

What is the impression produced by the sonnet upon us? Impressions of this sort are hard to define: but here one seems to be predominant and recognizable.

We receive an impression of excitement so intense that the declared and actual subject of the poem is as it were dissolved away by it. It is almost impossible not to forget that it is all about a book— Chapman's translation of *Homer*. There is a direct communication of emotion, which grows swifter and swifter, till in the final picture of Cortez, half visual, half abstract, it touches a consummation: the image is not merely stamped upon our minds by the emotional force of the poem, but the image gathers up, clinches, makes tangible, the emotional content of the poem. Cortez on the peak—it is the perfect culmination of the sonnet. All that the sonnet really means is crammed into that final image: it is the flower of the plant, the purpose and the essence of the created thing.

Let us leave this for a moment and examine the sonnet more coldly, putting aside, if we can, the immediate and overwhelming impression. We observe that the imagery of exploration and discovery is maintained from the beginning.

> Much have I *travell'd* in the realms of gold,
> And many goodly states and kingdoms seen;

> Round many western islands have I been...
> Oft of one wide expanse had I been told ...

From the first line the poet is a traveller, an explorer, voyaging among islands, discovering the realms of gold: he hears on his travels persistent rumours and reports of a great *El dorado*. The word of the conquistadors is helpful; for the phrase 'the realms of gold' is become so familiar, so much a part of current speech, that we forget that when Keats used it it was original. And it had come, I fancy, from the same reading whence came his picture of Cortez. *'El dorado'* means simply 'the realm, or the city, of gold'. Keats was, to his own mind, a conquistador, with Chapman's *Homer* for his new-found land.

In the first two lines of the sestet:

> Then felt I like some watcher of the skies
> When a new planet swims into his ken,

the imagery is slightly changed—he becomes the explorer not of earth but of heaven—an astronomer who has discovered a new planet; but the change, instead of weakening the poem, quite definitely strengthens and enriches it: it gives an infinite extension to its imaginative scope—to the yet unlimited earth the illimitable heavens are added, and by the exquisite use of the word 'swims' is created an impression of ethereal stillness, a background of quiet translunary spaces, against which the figure of Cortez on his peak emerges with craggy definition.

So that, on a closer examination, the immediate impression that the image of Cortez on the peak in Darien is the natural and, so to say, organic culmination of the poem, is fully substantiated. At the very outset Keats imagines himself as the explorer in search of *El dorado*, and when finally he likens himself to the mightiest of the conquistadors, at the supreme moment of discovery, he has carried the imagery with which he began to the pinnacle of its potentialities.

It is one of the greatest sonnets in the English language: its immediate effect is startling, and perhaps this cold-blooded analysis has yielded some reason why this is so. The unity of the poem lies deep and is *organic*: in the first line the last is implicit, as a flower is implicit in a seed. And this unity is achieved by what appears, on still closer examination, an almost miraculous subtlety.

Considered in its imagery alone, as we have seen, the poem is a perfect whole—one single and complex metaphor, as intricate as it is clear. There is a real progression, as it were a crescendo, of the imagery which seems to grow out of itself. It completely satisfies Keats's own demand upon poetry which he formulated eighteen months later.

> The rise, the progress, the setting of Imagery should, like the Sun come natural to him [the reader] shine over him and set soberly

although in magnificence leaving him in the Luxury of twilight. . . .

And we may take 'the progress and the setting of Imagery' in this sonnet as a concrete example of Coleridge's penetrating, but more intellectual *dictum*, which is so often misinterpreted:

> Images, however faithfully copied from Nature, and as acurately represented in words, do not of themselves characterize the poet. They become proofs of original genius only so far as they are modified by a predominant passion, or by associated thoughts and images awakened by that passion.

That is to say, imagery must not assume a *raison d'être* of its own; it must exist, not for its own sake, but as subordinated to the predominant emotion, which it has at once to obey, to express and to communicate. Only in so far as it does this will it, in Keats's words, 'come natural to the reader': otherwise it will merely distract him. In other words, on the side of the poet the imagery and the emotion must be one: 'rise, progress, and set' together in a perfect accord. . . . The unity of imagery and emotion is remarkable: in the octave, the imagery and emotion of eager exploration; in the sestet, the imagery and emotion of breathless discovery. The rhythm of the imagery precisely corresponds to the rhythm of emotion: and with a wonderful subtlety. . . . The octave and the sestet have each their separate crescendo. The rhythm of imagery and emotion of the whole sonnet is reduplicated in either part. In the first the silence of eager expectation and impotent surmise is triumphantly broken by

Till I heard Chapman speak out loud and bold;

in the second, where a repetition of the actual effect is impossible, because Chapman's *Homer* has been discovered and the discovery cannot be undone, its equivalent is nevertheless compassed by a master-stroke of intuitive genius, by a sort of imaginative parallelism. The silence of infinite space is first suggested, and against that silence absolute the silence of Cortez sounds like a thundercrash. . . .

[Middleton Murry then examines Keats's experiences and the poems he was writing in the months before this sonnet was composed].

The composition of a *great* poem is but a final conscious act supervening upon a long process of unconscious elaboration.

Can we, with the help of our evidence, more clearly define the nature of this process? What elements can we distinguish in it?

First and foremost, a predominant, constantly recurring complex of thought and emotion. Throughout the period of unconscious elabor-

ation Keats had been continually discovering more and more of what
was to him the highest reality: Nature, Poetry, the Nature of Poetry;
and the continual discovery was accompanied by an incessant emotional excitement. Whether his successive acts of discovery can properly be called 'thoughts' will depend upon the philosophy of the man
describing them, but 'thoughts' they shall be for us, as they were for
Keats:

> There came
> Thought after thought to nourish up the flame
> Within my breast . . .

These successive thoughts (which some would call intuitions), accompanied by an incessant emotional excitement, form what Coleridge
calls 'a predominant passion'—more exactly a persistent process of
thought-emotion.

Second, in the service of this persistent thought-emotion the specific
poetic-creative faculty has been continually at work to find means of
expression for it. These means of expression are chiefly images derived
from a series of particular sense-perceptions. Thus, the poet's first
perception of the moon:

> Lovely the moon in ether, all alone

is refined to a subtler perception of her

> Lifting her silver rim
> Above a cloud, and with a gradual swim
> Coming into the blue with all her light.

And this sense-perception is used to enable the poet to grasp his own
thought of the nature of poetry. The smooth and lovely motion of the
moon is a quality of the poetry he conceives:

> More strange, more beautiful, more smooth, more regal
> Than wings of swans, than doves, than dim-seen eagle.

So the image of the moon becomes an image of his thought of poetry.

Again, he sees the sea for the first time, and that perception of the
sea, with its attendant emotion, enables him once again to grasp his
main thought with its emotion. The image of the vast ocean also becomes an image of his vast 'idea' of poetry. Nay more, the very sound
of the sea,

> which whoso hears
> Must think on what will be, and what has been,

enables him to make audible, as the sight of the sea to make visible his thought. Again, another aspect of his thought is grasped through the vision of himself standing alone on a cliff (at Margate) or on a hill (at Hampstead), staring with wondering eyes at the prospect before him. He is 'a spirit standing apart upon the forehead of the age to come'.

So the poet's mind has been accumulating through successive acts of sense-perception a series of images which can be assimilated into the main process of his thought and act as surrogates for it. And the condition of this assimilation is an emotional and qualitative correspondence. His perception of the moon is a delighted discovery, so is his perception of the ocean—in both the hidden loveliness of an unknown reality is revealed to him; therefore, both in the qualities discovered and in the emotion awakened in discovering them, these sense-discoveries are analogous to the main thought—discovery of the nature of poetry. With his senses he discovers Nature, with his thoughts he discovers the nature of poetry.

His two crowning sense-discoveries were those of the moon and sea, and those are instantly pressed into the service of his thought: the images of the moon and the ocean can serve at will to embody the objects of his thought. And he is able to think more exactly concerning the nature of poetry because the sensuous images of moon and ocean are become true symbols of the reality about which he is thinking. So that in the process of unconscious elaboration the continually progressing thought is given ever fresh definition and substance by the images it is able to assimilate; and, on the other hand, the images acquire a thought-content. The thought steadily gains focus and intensity; the images significance.

Suddenly this complex of thought and images, which is working itself towards an organic unity, is ejected into poetic form. What occasions this sudden birth? The dominant thought, with its attendant emotion, is given a final focus by a particular event. The discovery of the nature of poetry, which had been going on for months, is consummated by the discovery of Chapman's *Homer*. Utterance becomes urgent, necessary, inevitable. The means are at hand—images long since assimilated to that dominant thought-emotion, of which the discovery of Chapman is the final instance and occasion.

But there is a final creative act. If this unconscious preparation were all, we should imagine Keats in his sestet saying: 'Then felt I —as I did when I discovered the moon, as I did when I discovered the ocean.' But the moon was discovered long ago, and so was the ocean. It will not do. It must be: 'Then felt I—as a man who discovers a new planet, as a man who discovers a new ocean.' Then to his need came the memory of Robertson's *America*, which he had read as a schoolboy. An inexact memory—for as Tennyson pointed out, it was Balboa, not Cortez, who stared at the Pacific—but one definite enough to give the final perfection to his imagery. . . .

From *Keats*, 4th Edition, Farrar, Straus & Giroux, Inc., New York, 1955. (First Edition, London, 1930, was entitled *Studies in Keats.*) These extracts have been taken from Chapter IV.

. . . The common cognomen of this world among the misguided and superstitious is 'a vale of tears' from which we are to be redeemed by a certain arbitary interposition of God and taken to Heaven—What a little circumscribe[d] straightened notion! Call the world if you Please "The vale of Soul-making" Then you will find out the use of the world (I am speaking now in the highest terms for human nature admitting it to be immortal which I will here take for granted for the purpose of showing a thought which has struck me concerning it) I say 'Soul making' Soul as distinguished from an Intelligence— There may be intelligences or sparks of the divinity in millions— but they are not Souls ⟨the⟩ till they acquire identities, till each one is personally itself. I[n]telligences are atoms of perception—they know and they see and they are pure, in short they are God—how then are Souls to be made? How then are these sparks which are God to have identity given them—so as ever to possess a bliss peculiar to each ones individual existence? How, but by the medium of a world like this? . . . I will call the word *a School instituted for the purpose of teaching little children to read—I will call the* human heart *the* horn Book *used in that School—and I will call the* Child able to read, the Soul *made from that* school *and its* hornbook. *Do you not see how necessary a World of Pains and troubles is to school an Intelligence and make it a soul? A Place where the heart must feel and suffer in a thousand diverse ways! Not merely is the Heart a Hornbook, It is the Minds Bible, it is the Minds experience, it is the teat from which the Mind or intelligence sucks its identity—As various as the Lives of Men are—so various become their souls, and thus does God make individual beings, Souls, Identical Souls of the sparks of his own essence—This appears to me a faint sketch of a system of Salvation which does not affront our reason and humanity. . . .*

(John Keats to George and Georgiana Keats, April 21, 1819)

AILEEN WARD

Endymion

... A MIRACLE occurs: the dark maiden is transformed into the bright haired goddess before his very eyes. The love of his dreams has become real at last, and they vanish into the forest together, leaving Peona lost in wonder.

This miraculous ending to a miraculous tale has left many readers as bewildered as Peona herself. Unwilling to take the poem as meaning what it seems to say, most of Keats's critics have moralized it into an allegory of a kind of supersexual love for a supersensuous beauty. Thus Endymion's wanderings become the quest of the poetic soul for 'communion with the ideal', and his agonized vacillation between the maiden and the goddess, and the final change of the one into the other, are taken to indicate the seeming conflict and ultimate harmony of the actual beauties of this world with ideal Beauty. Yet this interpretation is hardly convincing. The texture of the poem itself, so richly sensuous and unabashedly sensual, not merely obscures such a meaning, it contradicts it. Moreover, Keats at twenty-one, with his distrust of 'consequitive reasoning' and his hunger for 'a life of Sensations rather than of Thoughts', was not the kind of young man to prefer abstractions to realities, or the kind of poet to contrive an allegorical system. Indeed, as he later admitted, the development of his tale was 'uncertain', lacking a clear plan from the start.

Just as Keats never mentioned an allegory in discussing *Endymion* with his friends, so none of his first readers found any hint of allegory in the poem—not surprisingly, for the allegorical tradition was dead in Keats's time, even for readers of Spenser. Those who enjoyed the poem praised it chiefly for the imagery and accepted the metamorphosis of the Indian maid as the proper fairy-tale ending of a romance. Only Jeffrey in *The Edinburgh Review* sensed Keats's real innovation—to have given the familiar mythological figures 'an original character and distinct individuality', that is, a human significance; only Bailey suspected a hidden meaning in the action, which he could not believe Keats really intended: its approach 'to that abominable principle of *Shelley's*—that *Sensual Love* is the principle of *things*'.

This suggests why, in the increasingly literal-minded and prudish age of Tennyson, when the fairy-tale ending was no longer readily accepted, a Victorian lady critic found it necessary to invent the moralistic allegory to disguise Keats's naked meaning. For the poem is about sensual love, like most poems by men of twenty-one. Endymion represents not the poetic soul but the ideal lover; his adventures are an assertion of 'the holiness of the Heart's affections', and it is only because the poem expresses such an exalted idea of sexual love that the Victorian critics felt his quest must have another goal.

But if there is no allegory in *Endymion*, there is clearly a symbolic significance, one inherent in the events themselves, not imposed on them from without, which might be defined simply as the young man's discovery of the true nature of love. Keats himself seems to have discovered his full meaning only gradually, in the very act of writing. He started with 'a thing of beauty', and, like Adam in his dream, 'awoke to find it truth'. Sexual love, as Endymion describes it near the end of the first book, is the highest reach of happiness, the richest form of 'blending pleasurable', that most completely annuls the division between the self and the world outside; as such, it is the crown of all other values and the worthiest goal of our strivings. But even as Endymion set out on his quest of 'endless bliss', Keats's own ideas on the nature of love were changing. His new-won independence of Hunt, his deepened understanding of Shakespeare, his friendship with Bailey, his growing sense of tender responsibility for his young sister, his adventure—whatever it amounted to—with Isabella Jones, the disillusionments of the autumn, all these profoundly altered the naïve idealism with which he had begun. By the time he reached the fourth book, he had come to see the 'immortality of passion' which Endymion pursues as the hollow unreality that it is. And so an astonishing inversion of the legend takes place. The hero, on the point of winning his goddess, apparently betrays her; he wins her in the end only after renouncing her, and not in her own identity but by discovering her in a mortal maiden. It is hard not to believe that this unexpected turn of plot was deeply influenced by Keats's own emotional reversals of the fall. For up till the very end Endymion's progress parallels Keats's own feelings as he recorded them in his letters of October and November—disillusionment, depression, recovery; his loss of faith in the certainty of happiness, his renunciation of idealism, his discovery that the setting sun could put him to rights.

What of the ending, then? Is it a mere contrivance, a wrenching of the psychological narrative back to the foregone mythological conclusion? Partly so; or rather, the dénouement is presented in highly ambiguous terms and can be read in two quite different ways.[1] On the first, or mythological level, the maid is merely the goddess in a disguise which she has adopted to test Endymion's fidelity—a familiar fairy-tale device which Keats may have borrowed from a version of the legend in one of his Elizabethan poets. So when Endymion seems to renounce human love in reasserting his devotion to 'things of light', the maiden turns back into the goddess and rewards him with the 'immortality of passion' promised in the myth. On the second, the psychological or symbolic level, the maid represents a new conception of human love, far higher than Endymion's adolescent dream of 'endless bliss'. So when he finally realizes that to renounce the maid is to deny life itself, he is rewarded by the maid's transformation into the goddess; that is, real love, when accepted for the good it contains, leads to the fulfilment Endymion has sought all along. The ambiguity is inescapable; Keats's legend pulled him in one direction, his experience in another. As between the two interpretations, however, it seems clear that he gravitated towards the second, the human rather than the magical meaning. The last lines of the poem announce that Endymion has been 'spiritualiz'd' by 'some unlook'd for change' in his final adventure; and—what is not usually noticed—Cynthia herself has changed during the course of the story. She has surmounted her 'foolish fear' of yielding to a mortal lover and defied the 'decrees of fate' that doomed her to eternal chastity; she has been humanized, has learned to 'throw the goddess off', as Keats put it in a later poem, and 'play the woman's part'. Endymion meanwhile has been spiritualized in a most unexpected fashion by his encounter with the maid, for he wins his goddess at last not through his earlier acts of valour or disinterested sympathy but by learning to love another human being.

Keats's implication, taken in the context of his time, is audacious. He is saying that a man is spiritualized not by self-denial but by self-fulfilment: that a lover becomes perfect in love not by chastity but by the gradual realization of his passionate nature. He gives a hint of this in the first book, in his praise of sexual love as 'the chief intensity', the most 'self-destroying' of entanglements. This outgoing of the spirit into the identities of others is first experienced in response to the beauties of nature—the intense but ethereal pleasures of boyhood, when

> every sense
> Of mine was once made perfect in these woods.

---

[1] Two crucial lines near the end of Book IV are both capable of a double interpretation. In lines 957–58 Endymion may be renouncing either the Indian maid or his recent vow to lead a hermit's life; in lines 975–76 he may be either defying the fate which bars him from the maid or protesting against the fate of mortality which he has incurred through loving her.

Fresh breezes, bowery lawns, and innocent floods,
Ripe fruits, and lonely couch, contentment gave.

But with the advent of sexual longing this emotional self-sufficiency breaks down. Endymion's simple delights give way to troubled dreams, his boyish ambitions are forgotten in 'ardent listlessness'. Significantly, he begins his ascent toward love by plunging into the depths of the earth and exploring its 'silent mysteries' alone and in darkness. The meaning of his new need becomes clearer to him as he observes other lovers and learns to give of himself in friendship. But his rapturous dreams of an ideal love are followed by desolate awakenings, and often he longs to return to 'the old garden-ground of boyish days'. His first actual experience of love with the Indian maid seems a betrayal of his dreams; thus he can love her with only 'half [his] soul', and discovers in this conflict his painful lack of 'identity'. When at last he gives up the dream for the reality and acknowledges the fact of human incompleteness, he finds the 'self-destroying' completion through another that lies beyond it. So by loving first in guilt and confusion, then with greater understanding and self-acceptance, he is at last 'spiritualized' and wins his goddess as the legend promised.

Keats's search for a truth underlying 'the bare circumstance' of his legend is the real significance of *Endymion*. He was the first English poet to sense the possibility of a human meaning implicit in the myths themselves, rather than to fit them into a preconceived allegorical pattern, as in general the Elizabethans did, or merely to use them for decorative effect, like the eighteenth-century poets. His revolutionary attempt—if not his actual achievement—was, as Jeffrey implied, to suggest that the Greek myths were as relevant to our inner experience as the Christian myth was to Milton in an age when the pagan gods had lost their hold on men's imaginations. *Endymion* is a 'Song of Innocence and Experience' transposed into the mythic mode. Through Endymion's adventures Keats attempted to state, however gropingly, his belief in the necessity of growth, the value of the progression into experience, the impossibility of regression into innocence, the goal of a more complex harmony of being. The originality of his attempt becomes clear if *Endymion* is viewed against the literary conventions of his time. In romantic fiction, it has been pointed out, the polarities of sexual experience—lawful and lustful, tender and sensual, familial and alien—were usually represented by two heroines, a fair and a dark lady; and the hero, when forced to choose between them, invariably renounced his dark and passionate mistress for his innocent fair-haired love. Keats from the beginning blends these opposites: the bright-haired goddess appears to Endymion by night, the dark maiden by day; and in the end, by ambiguously wedding himself 'to things of light', Endymion chooses both women, as one is transformed into the other. In bringing the two parts of his own nature together, he becomes 'whole in love' and finds the object of his love has become whole for him.

Still the conflict between Keats's first and final intentions remains embedded within *Endymion*, and he apparently soon became aware of this. The doubts he expressed in September grew deeper. The following January, in the midst of revising the poem, he described it ironically to Haydon as 'deep and sentimental'; in February he told Taylor, 'I am anxious to get Endymion printed that I may forget it and proceed.' By April this weariness had turned into profound dissatisfaction. As he admitted with fanatical candour in the preface he wrote at this time, 'There is not a fiercer hell than the failure in a great object.' The chief fault of the poem, he realized, was the inexperience of life underlying the original conception. 'The imagination of a boy is healthy,' he wrote, 'and the mature imagination of a man is healthy; but there is a space of life between, in which the soul is in a ferment, the character undecided, the way of life uncertain, the ambition thick-sighted'—and from this sprang the 'mawkishness' which he castigated in what is surely the most extraordinary preface any author has written to any poem.

Yet for all its obvious faults of immaturity, *Endymion* is a uniquely interesting work, a Lucretian hymn to the vital force that creates beauty and heroism and love along with life itself, a young man's poem about a central experience of young manhood. Inevitably, and from the very time it was published, it has been compared to Shakespeare's *Venus and Adonis. Endymion* lacks the verbal control and dramatic power of the earlier work; but Shakespeare was twenty-eight when he wrote his first long poem, Keats was twenty-one. He was handicapped not only by his youth but by the sentimental tradition of his time, which left him no acceptable idiom for dealing forthrightly, as Shakespeare could, with physical love, at the same time that it led him to set a much more complex valuation on it. For better, for worse, *Endymion* is a work of romantic art.

And the final value of the poem is a peculiarly romantic one—its value to the poet himself. *Endymion* represents almost half of the poetry Keats published in his lifetime, and occupied him through nearly one-fourth of his poetic career; writing it was a major factor in his creative development. Keats himself was the first to value the poem in this fashion, and this was all the value he eventually allowed it. 'It is as good as I had power to make it—by myself,' he wrote Hessey a year later. 'Had I been nervous about its being a perfect piece, & with that view asked advice, & trembled over every page, it would not have been written.' In the end, he saw, his having written it mattered more than what he had written, and for a significant reason: 'That which is creative must create itself.—In Endymion,' he added, 'I leaped headlong into the Sea, and thereby have become better acquainted with the Soundings, the quicksand, & the rocks, than if I had stayed upon the green shore, and piped a silly pipe, and took tea & comfortable advice.' *Endymion* made Keats a poet, whatever Keats made of *Endymion*. In the very experience of failure he discovered the truth of achievement: 'That which is creative must create itself.'

From *John Keats: The Making of a Poet*, The Viking Press, Inc., New York, 1963, pp. 141-6. All footnotes except one have been omitted. Title supplied by the editor.

. . . Since I last wrote I have reread Keats a little . . . He was, in my opinion, made to be a thinker, a critic, as much as a singer or artist of words. This can be seen in certain reflective passages, as the opening to Endymion *and others in his poems. These passages are the thoughts of a mind very ill instructed and in opposition; keenly sensible of wrongness in things established but unprovided with the principles to correct that by. Both his principles of art and his practice were in many things vicious, but he was correcting them, even eagerly; for* Lamia *one of his last works shews a deliberate change in manner from the style of* Endymion *and in fact goes too far in change and sacrifices things that had better have been kept. Of construction he knew nothing to the last: in this same* Lamia *he has a long introduction about Mercury, who is only brought in to disenchant Lamia and ought not to have been employed or else ought to be employed again. The story has a moral element or interest; Keats was aware of this and touches on it at times, but could make nothing of it; in fact the situation at the end is that the sage Apollonius does more harm than the witch herself had done—kills the hero; and Keats does not see that this implies one of two things, either some lesson of the terrible malice of evil which when it is checked drags down innocence in its own ruin or else the exposure of Pharisaic pretence in the wouldbe moralist. But then if I could have said this to Keats I feel sure he wd. have seen it. In due time he wd. have seen these things himself. . . .*

(Gerard Manley Hopkins to Coventry Patmore, May 6, 1888)

ROGER SHARROCK

Keats and the Young Lovers

KEATS is a poet who has always held an important place among the authors studied at school between the ages of fourteen and seventeen. The inexorable tide of literary revaluation that flowed out from Russell Square and Cambridge after 1920 has left many features of the school English curriculum totally unsubmerged, and one of them is the appreciation of Keats as a poet of verbal felicity and sensuous evocativeness. Freshmen still come up knowing more of Keats than of the metaphysicals or Pope, and finding him more accessible. This is because they have met him in the years of early adolescence when one first begins to enjoy poetry, though one's enjoyment is usually confined to an intoxicating pleasure in the sound of words and in the visual and other sensuous impressions they can create. Lines and short passages exhibiting this power to render sensation crowd into the mind:

> ... divine liquids come with odorous ooze
> Through the cool serpent-pipe refreshfully.

> Cool'd a long age in the deep-delvéd earth.

> The coming musk-rose, full of dewy wine,
>   The murmurous haunt of flies on summer eves.

> It keeps eternal whisperings around
> Desolate shores ...

Of course, Shakespeare and Marlowe and many other poets can provide for the reader this purely sensuous pleasure; but the distinguishing mark of Keats is that when it is derived from his work the reader may feel that this is the main quality his poems have to offer and that they have no deeper meaning beyond the stimulation of our senses by the rendering of full and exquisite sensation.

However there must always be a difference between what we expect from sensation and what from the poetic treatment of sensation; other-

wise, unless a criterion of pure mimicry were employed, it would always be preferable to savour the scents and appearances, the rounded
fruit, drowsy poppies, oozing cider-press and so on, of an autumn day,
to reading Keats's *Autumn,* which would then give a new turn to the
Platonic condemnation of what is but a shadow of a shade. But Keats
offers something much more serious and self-contained than a mere
hedonistic machine, a delightful word-model of certain sensory experiences. The vivid picturing is not separable from a valuing comment
implied by the concrete detail of his evocation. *Autumn* accumulates
particular sensations in order to present a complex atmosphere—in
fact, a spirit of autumn, and that is why the spirit is personified in
the second stanza:

> Drows'd with the fume of poppies, while thy hook
> Spares the next swath and all its twinéd flowers.

and this insight into the nature of fruitfulness serves in its turn, beyond the purely descriptive, as a statement about maturity, the autumn
of the mind and of the artist to which Keats aspires.

Critics have sometimes ignored this distinction between experience
and poetry; in any case, the attitude to sensuous experience in the
early Keats, at once yearning and cloying, has upset many tastes from
the *Quarterly* to Matthew Arnold and beyond:

> The soul is lost in pleasant smotherings ...
> O Chatterton how very sad thy fate!

These descents into cocksure banality or the mawkishly sentimental
seem equally bad, and the academic critic or professional reviewer,
with his English sixth sense for an error in class tone, enlists the aid
of biographical knowledge to make his indictment the more damning:
quite apart from the defects of his literary education, Keats was mast-
ered and enslaved by a pining, degrading lovesickness for a very ordinary girl who flirted with mustachioed officers a foot taller than he was
and caused him bitter distress.

Now Keats's modern defenders and expositors have eloquently
pleaded his cause against these charges of immaturity. Whether within the academy by Clarence D. Thorpe and C. L. Finney, or outside
it by Middleton Murry,[1] he has been taken more and more seriously
as a poet distinguished by his profound and anguished effort towards
self-development. He is commended for the rapidity with which he
outgrew his early mawkishness and gradually increased his control
over verse and language; he is seen, especially by Middleton Murry,
as having finally achieved a knowledge of himself and of the poetic

---

[1] John Middleton Murry, *Keats and Shakespeare,* 1925; Clarence D. Thorpe,
The Mind of John Keats, 1926; Claude Lee Finney, *The Evolution of Keats's
Poetry,* 1936.

life which enabled him to contemplate in a clear-eyed fashion the mystery of life and death and to communicate his insight.

But to excuse Keats from immaturity and at the same time to ask us to accept him as the supreme artist of growth and development is to take over the terminology of his adverse critics and therefore to share their error. The error is to assume that as a result of any sound development of his art and outlook Keats put away not merely childish things but all the impulses and interests of his youth; it is to equate adolescence with delinquency and to stoop to the present-day vulgarity which makes 'adult' generally admitted as a term of critical praise. A maturing attitude to literature should mean widening and deepening an original perception, not 'growing out of' it, which would imply the abandonment of what in Keats's phrase had been proved upon our pulses. Admittedly development and the strain towards it is everywhere in Keats: the faery forest of Spenserian romance is passed to reach a new understanding of Shakespearian tragedy, conceived as a purgatorial experience for the soul; the greater beauty of the Olympians succeeds the lesser beauty of the Titans; *Hyperion* itself has to undergo a revision which sets it in the more truthful framework of a personal vision. But even in the finest work of 1819 Keats never transcends the concern with immediacy that marks his poetry in the phase now branded as adolescent. The Odes are only a richer brooding over immediacy. Where the Jacobean poet could savour with an intellectual finality:

the poor benefit of a bewitching minute,

Keats felt all the poignancy and none of the poverty of the isolated moment of intense experience; all his poetry is haunted by the problem of how to retain or prolong the moment or how to reconcile it with the oppression of mortal life:

A sense of real things comes doubly strong,
And, like a muddy stream, would bear along
My soul to nothingness.

Any evidence that Keats solved his problem so as to be able to present a matured wisdom, call it negative capability or what you will, is to be found in snatches in the letters, and not at all in his poems.

What I wish to maintain, against both the denigrators of Keats and those who proclaim his maturity, is that he remains in his most characteristic works not just the supreme poet for adolescents, but supremely the adolescent poet. He appeals to the emotions where they are connected most closely with the immediate satisfaction of the senses; the appeal is most strongly concentrated on the emotions of immature sexual love, both powerfully sensual and intensely idealistic, a focus for all sorts of budding curiosity and aspiration. Because Keats was a very exceptional adolescent he was aware of the heady, feverish pressure of this youthful romantic sickness on his imagination; he describes it admirably in the Preface to *Endymion*:

> The imagination of a boy is healthy, and the mature imagination of a man is healthy; but there is a space of life between, in which the soul is in a ferment, the character undecided, the way of life uncertain, the ambition thick-sighted: thence proceeds mawkishness, and all the thousand bitters which those men I speak of must necessarily taste in going over the following pages.

He projects into poetry the desires and cravings, at once timid and passionate, of 'Mister John Keats five feet high';[2] the poems in which he writes about his youthful love, first love whether satisfied or frustrated, happy or tragic, are *Isabella, The Eve of St Agnes* and *Lamia*. They span the main working period and the *annus mirabilis*, and it is only *Lamia* that was written after his love affair with Fanny Brawne had begun; thus in the first two of these poems he is creating the facts and discoveries of first love out of his imagination. The kind of self-indulgence so richly and beautifully carried out in these poems is far removed from the impersonality of the poet of negative capability; it is also to be distinguished from the mere pouring out of personal emotion, since Keats is not by any means transcribing from his own experience but capturing by a supreme effort of the imagination love and the lover as he would wish them to be, and re-creating the truths of passion as he does so; in such a process self-indulgence is turned into a discipline.

Each of the three poems is a variation on the same basic theme. A pair of young lovers is set down in the middle of a cold and hostile adult world; the warm sincerity of their passion is contrasted with the unfeeling sterility of their elders who are engaged in the pursuit of power or family pride, or in submitting to the restraints of material prudence. They enjoy their brief happiness in a secret retreat, the 'bower of hyacinth and musk Unknown of any' where Lorenzo meets Isabella, or the chamber of Madeline situated far away from the hall where hostile kinsmen revel and reached 'Through many a dusky gallery', or the enchanted palace built for Lamia in Corinth. A whole series of minor contrasts between light and darkness, warmth and cold, rich colours and drab tones, youth and age, serve to develop in contrapuntal form the fundamental opposition between romantic love and its enemies.

The treatment of the basic theme differs considerably from poem to poem, so that a different blending of the same structural elements

[2] Cf. *Letters of John Keats*, ed. M. Buxton Forman, 2nd ed. 1935, pp. 192–3.

shifts the emotional emphasis in each case and produces a different attitude to romantic love. *Isabella* is a tragedy in which Lorenzo is murdered and Isabella dies of grief; *The Eve of St Agnes* alone of the three poems presents happy and fulfilled love, though even here the pair who are allowed to flee away into the storm are placed in time 'ages long ago' and it is 'an elfin storm from faery land' which effects their escape: their happiness is to some extent artistically distanced and framed as an ideal model of romantic love rather than a possible state (though warm and breathing in Madeline's bedroom, they have become 'phantoms' as they glide away). In *Lamia* an ambiguity enters which marks it off a little from the other two poems; the nature of Lamia, both woman and demon, proclaims a love that is both desirable and deceitful, and though there is present the same opposition of youthful passion and harsh adult values, the grown-up world is now shown to have reason on its side in the person of 'the sage, old Apollonius'; it may be deplored as the analytic and destructive discursive reason, but its truth is not denied.

These variations of emphasis, as well as producing very different comments on the nature of love, are related to very different types of narrative style. This is why what may seem a highly obvious thematic unity has been obscured by the varied emotional atmosphere created in each poem. An examination poem by poem reveals these different styles of narration and the attitudes they present, as the adolescent mind guesses and gropes its way into the world of love, posing at each stage the same question: how can romantic love be possible in a harsh grown-ups' world?

Of the three, *Isabella*, the earliest, remains furthest from the world of love; love is seen as the highest value and therefore the most fitting subject for poetry, but the poem that ensues is a self-conscious exercise in sentiment. In this connection it is interesting to see that Keats soon came to recognise the artificiality of its love-melancholy, attributing to it 'an amusing sober-sadness' and concluding that it was 'a weak-sided poem' only too 'smokeable' by the reviewers of the *Quarterly*.[3] Its manner, working through the slow and decorative stanza, is diffuse and luxuriant; a brief tragic tale from Boccaccio is presented at one remove so as to extract the last drop of sentimental pathos. The first embrace of the lovers reveals a view of life that would contain experience within the bounds of 'poesy':

> So said, his erewhile timid lips grew bold,
> And poesied with hers in dewy rhyme:
> Great bliss was with them, and great happiness
> Grew, like a lusty flower in June's caress.

[3] *Letters of John Keats*, ed. cit., p. 391.

The image suggests that the kiss exists in order that a poet may write about it; it also suggests that love is a mode of poetry conceived as a state of luxurious contemplation beyond the cares of the ordinary world. A graceful and accomplished artifice of sorrow is imposed on the story; there is a kind of self-conscious tuning-up of the poetry to make it equal to contain the theme:

> O Melancholy, linger here awhile!
> O Music, Music, breathe despondingly!
> O Echo, Echo, from some sombre isle,
> Unknown, Lethean, sigh to us—O sigh!

The method may be described as a rhetorical lyricism. There are frequent apostrophes like those above and those to 'sad Melpomene' and to 'eloquent and famed Boccaccio', and many highly mannered repetitions and declamations. The management of some of these rhetorical constructions is very beautiful, for instance, the description of Isabella's grief, a variation on the word 'forgot':

> And she forgot the stars, the moon, the sun,
> And she forgot the blue above the trees,
> And she forgot the dells where waters run,
> And she forgot the chilly autumn breeze:
> She had no knowledge when the day was done,
> And the new moon she saw not . . .

Sorrow is stylised like a mourning figure on an urn. The long declamatory passages disperse the emotion and cause it to cling to detached, pictorial moments of the story. A repetitive series of questions fruitlessly probes the origins of the brothers' commercial and family pride which has made them decide to dispose of their sister's lover ('Why were they proud? . . .'): this might seem an unwarranted digression in a tauter, less lyrical form of narrative; even the brilliant evocation of the Florentine capitalists' exploited slaves in every corner of the earth might seem to run away from the main narrative into vivid side-tracking word-pictures:

> For them the Ceylon diver held his breath
> And went all naked to the hungry shark.

and the tone of overwrought indignation seems equally to be at variance with or at least to complicate the emotional atmosphere already established. But in the pattern of balanced contrasts Keats has chosen for his form this digression on the materialism of the brothers provides the dark background of the uncomprehending adult world that is needed to throw into relief the pure unspoilt love of Lorenzo and Isabella; and the feverishly reiterated questions further make plain

that the young themselves cannot comprehend the motives behind the
crass misunderstanding of their elders.

All is distanced and softened. The slightly quaint mannerism of the
imagery contributes to the general effect of sentimental pathos not
so much contrived as tamed ('Isabella's cheek/Fell sick within the
rose's just domain'; 'those Baalites of pelf'). The intense and dramatic
prolepsis of:

> So the two brothers and their murder'd man
> Rode past fair Florence,

only serves, by reminding us of the starkly tragic narrative, to reveal
how much it has been transformed into a rhetorical lyric. Even the
ghastly business of the severed, loam-stained head and its morbid
retention is turned with great skill to favour and to prettiness.

To turn to *The Eve of St Agnes* is to pass from diffuseness to intensity; the narrative is again wrought up to the pitch of lyric in the
flow and throb of its emotion, but the method is richly descriptive, not
declamatory, and everything contributes to the isolation of the central
figures, splendid in their romantic passion against the dark background
of their elders' hatred, cold hearts in a cold season. Though apparently loaded with descriptive detail, evocation of the atmosphere of
the medieval castle, architectural fancies and the like, none of the
pictorial passages is merely decorative and all contribute to the perpetual tension between youth and age, life and death, warmth and
cold, that make up the musical harmony of the poem. Keats was clearly
inspired by the similar musical pattern in *Romeo and Juliet* and this
has not passed unnoticed;[4] 'Angela the old' recalls the Nurse; her
age and weakness is several times emphasised, until in the conclusion
she dies 'palsy-twitched with meagre face deform', and like Shakespeare's Nurse she has a coarse-mindedness which is ready to attribute
the worst motives to Porphyro's desire to be guided to Madeline's
room: the treatment of the Nurse in both works throws into relief
the pure ardour of the young lovers. The Beadsman too, 'meagre,
barefoot, wan', leads his life even further away from the sources of
love and passion, among the sculptured dead:

> Emprison'd in black purgatorial rails.

His appearance at the beginning of the poem provides for a double
contrast: first the silver snarling trumpets suddenly break upon this
universe of death and penance; they usher in a lively but unfeeling
and superficial world; it has colour but no inner life and is described
in words suggesting heraldic colours or armorial bearing ('argent

4 See R. K. Gordon, 'Notes on Keats's *Eve of St. Agnes*', *Modern Language
Review*, xli, 1946, pp. 413–19.

revelry') and some of its chief members are also old or deformed ('dwarfish Hildebrand', 'that old Lord Maurice, not a whit More tame for his gray hairs'). Then comes the genuine passion of Porphyro and Madeline; they and what belongs to them are described in rich natural colour terms, usually those of crimson and the rose:

> Sudden a thought came like a full-blown rose,
> Flushing his brow.

The stained glass of Madeline's casement is coloured like the wings of the tiger-moth and its emblazonings blush with the blood of queens and kings.

This is not the tentative calf-love of *Isabella* but a fully consummated passion. The lovers lie at the warm heart of the castle, secure from the physical and moral coldness outside; the poem is built up like a Ptolemaic universe of spheres: we move from the utter chill of the natural world, the hare in the frozen grass, to the Beadsman in the chapel, too old and austere for love, then to the revelry in the hall, and finally to the centre of this world of love, Madeline's room, her bed, and Madeline in it. There is then a movement outwards from the warm centre through the enclosing layers when the lovers escape into the night.

As it is the most artistically assured of these poems, so is the *Eve* the most confident statement of a happy and realised romantic love; only in the hint of fairy tale at the end is there any withdrawal of the poet from full sympathy to a more detached point of view. In *Lamia* the self-absorption of the lovers is exposed to a far more severe attack from the envy of the adult world. The critical spirit of Apollonius brings about the destruction of romantic passion. But its chief enemy is within; here a radical ambiguity appears, not present in the earlier poems. Love is seen as at once exquisite and fatal, not running into danger from external forces, but bearing the seeds of death within itself; it is not only fatal, but has about it a quality of corruption. Lamia is a demon as well as a woman.

The adolescent quest, shifting from poem to poem, for some way of establishing the values of passionate love in the hostile adult world, here meets with disillusion. But *Lamia* would be easier to understand if it were simply a poem on the recurring romantic theme of the fatal passion leading to madness and death, like *La Belle Dame Sans Merci*. However Keats still clings uneasily to the only hand-hold he has, though he sees it must give way. Lamia is both piteously beautiful and utterly false. Apollonius is at one and the same time the voice of truth and wisdom and a waspish disagreeable old pedant; in the structure of the poem he fills the role of Angela, the Beadsman, and Isabella's brothers in its predecessors. Keats sees truth itself as inimical to happi-

ness; romantic love is a personal discovery of value *and* a surrender to
phantoms:

> Do not all charms fly
> At the mere touch of cold philosophy?

The use of Newtonian science to illustrate the working of the adult
critical spirit is apt: the discursive reason cannot be contradicted,
but it entails an emotional impoverishment; after all, it is the work of
this 'cold philosophy', not the sweet falsehood of Lamia, which brings
about Lycius's death.

The imaginative intensity of these poems, particularly the *Eve,*
would not have been possible without the assumption that romantic
passion is the principal source of moral and spiritual values, because
it is most productive of moments of finely perceptive sympathy when
a 'sort of oneness' can be experienced. In his effort to ground human
life upon personal values Keats looks forward through a long succession of nineteenth century and modern writers. The world gives
neither certitude nor peace, then:

> Ah, love, let us be true
> To one another!

as Arnold says in *Dover Beach,* and the heroes and heroines of E. M.
Forster are saying the same thing in their search for happiness through
personal relations. Meanwhile at the popular level the modern myth
of romantic passion throws a huge shadow. It seems likely that these
youthful poems of Keats will remain the finest poetic expression of
the myth.

From *A Review of English Literature,* Edited by A. Norman
Jeffares, vol. II, no. I. January 1961, pp. 76–86.

---

*. . . I had not a dispute but a disquisition with Dilke, on various sub-
jects; several things dovetailed in my mind, & at once it struck me,
what quality went to form a Man of Achievement especially in
Literature & which Shakespeare posessed so enormously—I mean*
Negative Capability, *that is when man is capable of being in uncer-
tainties, Mysteries, doubts, without any irritable reaching after the
fact & reason—. . . with a great poet the sense of Beauty overcomes
every other consideration, or rather obliterates all consideration. . . .*
(John Keats to George and Tom Keats, December 21, 27, 1817)

JOHN HOLLOWAY

The Odes of Keats

In H. W. Garrod's book on Keats there is one sentence about Keats's Odes that is a good deal more pointed and significant than its author presumably intended. Our attention is drawn in it to 'the close connexions of thought which exist between all of the ... Odes with the exception of that *To Autumn* ... a sequence ... not of time but of mood'.[1] The reader's first reaction, perhaps, will be suspicion of that unremarked shift from 'thought' to 'mood'; his second, that if this is an evasion, it comes near to solving the difficulty it evades. What unites these poems is essentially a singleness in experience; and in a sense it it too elusive for the first word, but too considered, too developed, too much articulated for the second. Yet if the Odes really are a unified sequence, the best way to understand them fully is to treat them as such, and make them interpret each other. So far, this has hardly been done—in part because critics have been too ready to think (as Garrod did) that *To Autumn* stands quite by itself, and in part because they have thought *On Indolence* too bad to deserve much attention. These restrictions of interest are precipitate; and a more systematic inquiry not only offers a more sensitive, balanced, comprehensive interpretation of each poem by itself, but seems to do something in addition. It seems also to show that these poems collectively make up a psychological document—an unexpected one—of unique interest. To a great extent, they are actually about that part of Keats's mental life of most significance to both him and us. They prove to be a complex and detailed poetic revelation of what Keats knew himself as the creative mood. The present study, then, has a double purpose: to add to our insight into the Odes as poems, and to indicate just how much they reveal of Keats the writer.

Let us begin with the Ode *On Indolence,* though only because its language is baldest and simplest. To trace a genuinely chronological development through the Odes, it would be necessary to show, if we took this as a starting-point, that it was written first; and this may very well not be true, though the evidence is less conclusive than Miss

[1] H. W. Garrod, *Keats* (1926), p. 97.

Lowell, for example, seemed to think.[2] But my purpose is rather to identify, as definitely as can be done, a mood which seems to underlie all the Odes, and appears in them sometimes in a more, sometimes (and *On Indolence* is an example) in a less developed form. Besides this, however, Keats's *Letters* make it clear that on March 19, 1819 (at the beginning of the period in which all these poems were written) he was not only in the exact mood of *On Indolence,* but could almost paraphrase the poem in prose:

> ... This morning I am in a sort of temper indolent and supremely careless: I long after a stanza or two of Thompson's Castle of Indolence. My passions are all asleep from my having slumbered till nearly eleven and weakened the animal fibre all over to a delightful sensation about three degrees this side of faintness—if I had teeth of pearl and the breath of lillies I should call it langour—but as I am I must call it Laziness. In this state of effeminacy the fibres of the brain are relaxed in common with the rest of the body, and to such a happy degree that pleasure has no show of enticement and pain no unbearable frown. Neither Poetry, nor Ambition, nor Love have any alertness of countenance as they pass by me: they seem rather like three figures on a greek vase—a Man and two women whom no one but myself could distinguish in their disguisement. This is the only happiness; and it is a rare instance of advantage in the body overpowering the Mind.[3]

So much for prose. The poem could scarcely do more to convey the same ideas. Keats affirms that neither Love, Ambition nor Poetry has charm enough to tempt him from a mood of exquisite somnolence, when

> ... ripe was the drowsy hour
> The blissful cloud of summer indolence
> Benumbed my eyes.

Both pain and pleasure seem to vanish, and they leave only a simple sensuous awareness, calm and yet somehow keen:

> The open casement pressed a new-leav'd vine
> Let in the budding warmth and throstle's lay.

[2] A. Lowell, *John Keats,* II, p. 258.
[3] *Letters,* ed. M. B. Forman (2nd edition, 1935), p. 315. Miss D. Hewlett (*A Life of John Keats,* 2nd edition, p. 244) writes 'when he (Keats) wrote, or finished, the *Ode on Indolence* in May the man and two women ... became three female figures'. But while the poem is explicit that Love and Poesy are 'maidens' there is nothing to show that Keats is thinking of Ambition as female, and a little perhaps to show that he is not.

This is all plain enough. Keats's mood is not subtle or complex, and it does not develop in the course of the poem. What is significant is that several turns of phrase or thought in this Ode reappear in the others; and there are elements of something that is more complex and that does develop. Of these, the drowsy indolence is of course one; so is the idea that Ambition is worthless because coming

> From a man's little heart's short fever-fit.

The indolent mood which is the source of the poem, and somehow mingles sleeping and waking, is not lethargy but in some sense a visionary state; not devoid of pleasure and pain, but transmuting them:

> Pain had no sting, and pleasure's wreath no flower.

Pain and pleasure have not ceased entirely, but ceased only to be disturbances, superficial additions to life. Poetry, which seems for the moment only 'my demon Poesy', the strongest of temptations,

> has not a joy
> At least for me—so sweet as drowsy noons
> And evenings steeped in honey'd indolence.

And this indolence is a positive thing, bringing a calm pervasive happiness that—its crucial feature perhaps—seems near to a suspension of sense for some other more elusive but more illuminating kind of experience:

> O, why did ye not melt, and leave my sense
> Unhaunted quite of all but nothingness?

On Indolence seems at first to reject poetry, but it is really a poem about the mood from which Keats's poetry at that time sprang. That this was consciously in Keats's mind is to some extent confirmed by one of the sonnets *On Fame*, probably written at about this time:

> Fame like a wayward girl will still be coy
> To those who woo her with too slavish knees . . .
> Make your best bow to her and bid adieu
> Then if she likes it she will follow you.[4]

The *Ode To Psyche* clarifies the situation. Keats's mood here is much like the mood of *On Indolence*:

> Surely I dream't today, or did I see
> The winged Psyche with awaken'd eyes?
> I wandered in a forest thoughtlessly
> And, on the sudden, fainting with surprise
> Saw two fair creatures . . .

[4] *Letters*, p. 338 (April 30, 1819).

—here is the same inertia and oblivion and suspension between sleeping and waking. When he finds Cupid and the goddess 'in soft-handed slumber' together

> 'Mid hush'd cool-rooted flowers fragrant-eyed
> Blue, silver-white, and budded Tyrian
> They lay calm-breathing on the bedded grass

this is almost exactly like his own condition in *On Indolence*;[5] and the interaction between Keats's own emotions, and the emotions of his subject, will prove later to be an important aspect of the *Ode to a Nightingale*. Keats has a good phrase in *To Psyche* for the central quality of his feeling: 'this wide quietness'. But as the poem proceeds, drowsy numbness is raised, as it were, to a higher power of itself:

> I see, and sing, by my own eyes inspired.

Keats is inspired to sing through seeing the goddess (especially, one is sorry to say, through seeing her 'lucent fans'). He desires to serve the deity of a mood whose expression is more complex, more impassioned, and indeed more intellectual, than anything in *On Indolence*. His mood tends towards activity, it is a balanced tension of excitement, and here unmistakably it has something of an intellectual insight, a fuller understanding:

> . . . I will be thy priest, and build a fane
> In some untrodden region of my mind
> Where branched thoughts, new grown with pleasant pain
> . . . shall murmur.

> A rosy sanctuary will I dress
> With the wreath'd trellis of a working brain

> And there shall be for thee all soft delight
> That shadowy thought can win.

The stress falls largely on the melancholic aspects of Psyche the Love-goddess (she is called 'mournful Psyche' in *On Melancholy*); Keats laments that she has no

> . . . virgin-choir to make delicious moan
> Upon the midnight hours.

But the 'wide quietness' of this poem has a certain poignancy, and as the mood develops, Keats's tone becomes more complex and at the same time more incisive.

For all that, however, the genesis of the poem still lies in 'soft-

[5] . . . Ye cannot raise
My head cool-bedded from the flowery grass.

handed slumber'; and that this originates the whole sequence of experience is suggested once more at the beginning of the *Ode On Melancholy*. The oblivion of Lethe is too uncompromising, wolfsbane too powerful a narcotic, the death moth too grim and macabre to incarnate 'mournful Psyche'. These are extreme measures that the mood cannot survive:

> . . . shade to shade will call too drowsily
> And drown the wakeful anguish of the soul . . .

The 'melancholy fit' falls suddenly, like an April shower 'that fosters the droop-headed flowers all'; and like the shower, Melancholy has its own reviving virtue. In this mood we are to 'glut' sorrow in the contemplation of beautiful things, 'feed, deep, deep' on them; and that experience will also be an insight.

The last stanza suggests how. 'She dwells with Beauty—' whether 'she' is the imagined mistress, or the goddess of Melancholy, or both or either, leaves the sense unaffected. The experience of Beauty is a revelation; of Beauty's meaning, and also of its transience. Melancholy is developed here to a keener, tenser equipoise of sorrow and uncertainty, and also of exaltation and elusive understanding:

> . . . Beauty that must die;
> And Joy, whose hand is ever at his lips
> Bidding adieu; and aching Pleasure nigh
> Turning to poison while the bee-mouth sips:
> Ay, in the very temple of delight
> Veil'd Melancholy has her sovran shrine
> Though seen of none save him whose strenuous tongue
> Can burst Joy's grape against his palate fine:
> His soul shall taste the sadness of her might,
> And be among her cloudy trophies hung.

This is very different from the drowsy numbness of *Indolence*, and its 'strenuous tongue' is like the 'working brain' of *To Psyche*. But the last two lines have a special interest: 'cloudy trophies' may hint at the elusiveness of the insight that dwells with Beauty, but the cadence of this couplet causes it, and therefore the whole stanza, to exemplify what it describes. The reader watches Joy bidding adieu, because he is taken through the experience of which the poem gives an account.

Of these three Odes, *On Indolence* in the main portrays a mood which is the embryo of the 'melancholy fit', *To Psyche* celebrates the deity of one of its forms (love-melancholy), and *On Melancholy* displays its growth and intensity and climax. The other two—perhaps the other three—Odes centre upon particular things which have evoked or represented the experience for Keats himself. To a very

considerable degree they run parallel—though this has been over-
looked by several critics, or expressly denied; and they have many
features in common with the three Odes discussed so far. Thus in the
opening lines of *To a Nightingale* the drowsy numbness is, once more,
both an aching pain and a too-sharp happiness; hearing the song induces Keats to forget and also remember what is unhappy in life
—it brings oblivion that, at a deeper level, is keener knowledge. Once
again the senses are stilled, but to an 'embalmed darkness' that is even
so a heightened sensuous awareness divining the surrounding sensuous
wealth; and when Keats thinks of 'easeful Death' it is like 'nothingness'
in *On Indolence*—as the completion of this unique oblivion.

No one seems quite to have explained the imaginative movement
of the poem at the point where Keats makes the nightingale immortal.
Bridges regarded this passage as fanciful, and Miss Lowell as
Platonic.[6] Garrod, avoiding these errors, suggests that the nightingale
is immortal because Keats thinks of it as a Dryad.[7] But why is it appropriate to think the bird immortal for any reason? Why should we not
suppose ourselves confronted here with irresponsible, fanciful inge-
nuity? The answer is, perhaps, that at the climax of his poem Keats
rightly allows a new ease of movement within the set of ideas he is
controlling: he uses a freedom of combination which characterizes
poetry at high temperatures, as I believe it does chemistry (in both
cases, oddly enough, *constitutes* is perhaps an apter word). The nightingale momentarily assumes the qualities of that ecstasy which it
seems to experience, and which it induces in Keats. Within the apparently irresponsible movement of the stanza runs an exact line of what
I am almost tempted to call logical development. Keats, entranced as
he listens to the nightingale and responds to its apparent ecstasy, has
an experience that seems to him to transcend experience; and in this
stanza he claims that the nightingale's song is unrestricted by either
time or space—which after all are pervasive features of experience. The
voice of the nightingale, we might put it, is made immune first
to history, and then to geography: it can establish a *rapport* with
dead generations or with faery lands; and

> ... the same that oft-times hath
> Charm'd magic casements, opening on the foam
> Of perilous seas, in faery lands forlorn

is not Romantic escapsim or idle gesturing. Word by word, this passage, in the free way of poetry, is indicating the definite qualities of
what was for Keats something he knew: the magic, the 'wideness',

---

[6] *John Keats. A Critical Essay* (1895), quoted in Lowell, op. cit., II, p. 252
(Miss Lowell's own discussion of the poem).
[7] Op. cit., p. 114.

the heightened tension, the sadness, are things that we have by now traced elsewhere.

But like the *Ode On Melancholy*, this poem represents the experience it describes, and represents it without abridgement; it gives not only the genesis and progress and climax, but also the dissolution, of the mood that seems central to all the Odes. Garrod's belief[8] that at this point Keats's poem may have owed something to Wordsworth's *Solitary Reaper* is probably correct; but it leads him to say of

> . . . thy plaintive anthem fades

that it is 'the only false note which the Ode discovers'. Here a too full knowledge of the psychology of composition appears to have confused a quite separate question of criticism; reading this poem in the light of the other Odes makes it clear that 'plaintive' is here no false but the exactly right note. If it were false, so would be 'faery lands forlorn'. Forlorn they might be, but they would then intrude. They do not, because as ever the magic dissolves in its own moment of existence:

> Turning to poison while the bee-mouth sips

—and the very last words of the poem, with their uncertainty between waking and sleeping, are not in opposition to what has gone before, but express something that is integral to the situation, and that has appeared in every Ode so far. The poem has reverted from its climax to a calmer mood not altogether remote from the mood of its origin.

Garrod and Miss Lowell have both assumed a contrast between *To a Nightingale* and *On a Grecian Urn*.[9] Miss Lowell sees a 'direct antithesis'; Garrod describes *On a Grecian Urn* as written in 'strong revulsion' from the mood of *On Melancholy,* and of this poem as in fairly close sympathy with *To a Nightingale*. But it is rather doubtful whether the difference is more than a shift of emphasis. Miss Lowell's account, 'realization of the eternal quality of art binds and heals the bitter wounds incident upon mere living', suggests that *On a Grecian Urn* is a vicarious *exegi monumentum*. Garrod's view is not unlike this: 'the *Grecian Urn* presents . . . the world of beauty and human passions, only fixed by art.' He speaks of its 'rather formal philosophy'. 'The theme of . . . (the first four stanzas) . . . is the arrest of beauty, the fixity given by art to forms which in life are fluid and impermanent, and the appeal of art from the senses to the spirit. The theme of the final stanza is the relation of beauty to truth, to thought.' These views distort the poem. It has no 'rather formal philosophy'. It as much expresses a mood as *To a Nightingale*; but the mood is modulated to

[8] Op. cit., p. 115.
[9] Garrod, op. cit., p. 104, 108; Lowell, op. cit., II, p. 247.

the different object which inspires it. Between the nightingale and the urn is the difference of embalmed darkness and perpetual spring or summer; but 'Veil'd Melancholy' is never wholly absent from *On a Grecian Urn*, though too much veiled, it seems, for some critics. There is a hint of her even in the 'maidens loth' and 'struggle to escape' and the 'wild ecstasy' of the first stanza; in the second comes the eternal frustration of the dancers; their eternal freedom, in the third, perhaps makes the poet happy in sympathy, but it is happiness that trembles upon passionate regret; stanza four contrasts the eternal grace of the figures and the eternal silence and desolation of their 'little town'; and the last stanza contrasts the kindly wisdom of the urn with the waste and frustration of ordinary life. Throughout the poem, then, this antithesis is maintained. The lovers and the musicians are protected from humanity's disillusionments only through being denied its rewards. Their triumph, so far as they have one, is in the realized perfection of a single poignant and yet gracious moment. This moment embraces the same fusion of quiet ('thou still unravished bride of quietness') and wild ecstasy, the same exquisite but precarious balance of grief and happiness, the same eternalization of a passing moment, that Keats himself knew in *To a Nightingale*. In *On a Grecian Urn* he is describing, as he sees it in others, what in the former poem he experienced and expressed for himself. The experience is not, of course, identical; but the type is unchanged. Keats is now the recorder, in the other poem he was the protagonist. It would simplify to say that this was a full account. The nightingale was also in ecstasy, and to some extent the loneliness of the little town and the dancer's raptures are contagious. But the urn-figures are a fuller manifestation of this rapture than the nightingale, and there is a different balance in the two poems between the poet's own mood and the object evoking it.

Garrod was critical of the words 'cold pastoral', as a departure from all that had gone before.[10] but they are, on the contrary, an exact continuation. The sculpted pipes play 'ditties of no tone' to the mind's ear only; and this coldness is not the source only in plain fact of the dancer's ecstatic permanence, for it evokes also something that is central to that ecstasy. Cleanth Brooks's account, 'the scene is one of violent love-making',[11] is to say the least of it premature; it ignores the subtlety and elaboration of Keats's scene, and how carefully (even before we reach the altar and the priest) he marshalls the imaginative elements which make the whole poem, and nothing less than that, explain those so-much-discussed closing lines. He does this once again in saying that the urn can 'tease us out of thought *As doth eternity*': it leads, not to no thought, but to a unique kind of thought. And when Cleanth Brooks writes that the urn says 'imaginative insight embodies

[10] Op. cit., p. 106.   [11] *The Well-Wrought Urn*, p. 143.

the basic and fundamental perception... the urn is beautiful, and yet its beauty is based ... on an imaginative perception of essentials'[12] no doubt he is right. This does summarize, in abstract form, what Keats told his reader in the concrete form of poetry. But to gloss this with 'mere accumulations of facts ... are meaningless' is to get away from the poem again. Keats glossed it by writing the whole Ode to convey what he thought an imaginative perception of essentials was like. A kind of peace, a kind of excitement, a kind of regret, a kind of ecstasy, an insight that seemed central and yet was strangely like oblivion—the list may briefly remind the successful reader of what he found in the poem, but prose, of course, must say obscurely what poetry says clearly.

There is one poem of Keats which throws light of particular importance on the Odes. This is the sonnet 'Why did I laugh tonight?' which we know, from the *Letters,* must have been written shortly before March 19, 1819, and therefore near the beginning of this creative period. It is important for three reasons: it hints at some of the antinomies which the present enquiry has emphasized, it declares that ecstasy is inseparable from physical experience, which we saw Keats recognizing as the embryo of *On Indolence,* and it has verbal parallels with no less than three of the Odes. 'Nothing ever becomes real until it is experienced' Keats writes, immediately before copying out this poem for George and Georgiana Keats.[13] And then:

> Why did I laugh tonight? No voice can tell:
> No God no Deamon of severe response
> Designs to reply from Heaven or from Hell.—
> Then to my human heart I turn at once—
> Heart! thou and I are here sad and alone;
> Say, wherefore did I laugh? O mortal pain!
> O Darkness! Darkness! ever must I moan
> To question Heaven and Hell and Heart in vain!
> Why did I laugh? I know this being's lease
> My fancy to its utmost blisses spreads:
> Yet could I on this very midnight cease
> And the world's gaudy ensigns see in shreds.
> Verse, fame and Beauty are intense indeed
> But Death intenser—Death is Life's high mead.

Lines 9-10 repeat, perhaps rather obscurely, the 'advantage in the body overpowering the mind' which Keats referred to in describing his indolent mood of March 19th; and it has often been noted how line 11 resembles 'to cease upon the midnight with no pain' of *To a Night-*

---

[12] *The Well-Wrought Urn*, p. 150.   [13] *Letters*, p. 316.

ingale. But critics have not usually noticed that the gaudy ensigns in shreds have clearly something in common with the 'cloudy trophies' of *On Melancholy* (though the two images are put almost to contrary uses in the two poems); and, more important, that the 'Verse, fame and Beauty' of line 13 are virtually the same as the Poetry, Ambition and Love of *On Indolence*. Both by its wording and by its substance, therefore, this sonnet does something further to suggest that the Odes explore various phases of a single experience.

Any similar suggestion about *To Autumn* must be very tentative. Keats composed the other poems within a brief period in the spring and early summer of 1819, and this not until several months later. It may well have arisen from a quite independent poetic impulse. But it is not altogether fanciful, perhaps, to see it as a quiet and gentle close to the whole sequence of poems, standing to them all somewhat as the last three lines of *On a Grecian Urn* stand to that single poem. Nor would it be difficult to point out details that are reminiscent of the Odes—Autumn drowsing with the fumes of poppies (drowsing, too, among the 'twined flowers', like Keats himself in *On Indolence* or the goddess in *To Psyche*), or Keats's rejection of the songs of spring, or perhaps even the mourning choirs of gnats. But however this may be, stressing the affinity serves one indisputably useful purpose: it shows that *To Autumn* is totally different from the descriptive poem of a catalogue kind. Keats has given in it a quite selective picture of autumn, and one that conveys a quite distinctive mood. How far the earlier poems have made us familiar with the analogues of this mood is perhaps an open question.

All in all, Miss Lowell was rash to say, of *On Indolence*, 'this, of course, was pure fatigue'.[14] It seems much more like an expression of the very frame of mind from which at this time, to varying degrees on various occasions, Keats found the raptures of poetic inspiration generate themselves—and do so, moreover, exactly because he was not seeking them. The other Odes document various aspects of this process of generation. Sir Maurice Bowra, writing 'the three stanzas in which Keats tells of the timeless moments depicted on the Urn arise from his own knowledge of what creation is'[15] seems to suggest this also. And there are, of course, well-known passages in Keats's *Letters* which indicate that he regarded what might be called the embryonic condition of the mood conveyed by these poems as also the embryo of poetic inspiration. 'As to the poetical Character itself (I mean that sort of which, if I am anything, I am a Member...) it has no self—it is everything and nothing—it has no character—it enjoys light and shade';[16] 'if Poetry comes not as naturally as the Leaves on a tree it had

[14] Op. cit., II, p. 258.   [16] *Letters*, p. 227 (October 27, 1818).
[15] *The Romantic Imagination*, p. 142.

better not come at all'.[17] In a word, the Odes are not only products of what Keats himself called 'Negative Capability', but taken together are a uniquely full account of what it is like and how it develops.

From *The Cambridge Journal*, vol. V, April 1952, pp. 416–25.

[17] Ibid., p. 108 (February 27, 1818).

...I am certain of nothing but of the holiness of the Heart's affections and the truth of Imagination—What the imagination seizes as Beauty must be truth—whether it existed before or not—for I have the same Idea of all our Passions as of Love they are all in their sublime, creative of essential Beauty.... The Imagination may be compared to Adam's dream—he awoke and found it truth. I am the more zealous in this affair, because I have never yet been able to perceive how any thing can be known for truth by consequitive reasoning... we shall enjoy ourselves here after by having what we called happiness on Earth repeated in a finer tone and so repeated—And yet such a fate can only befall those who delight in sensation rather than hunger as you do after Truth—Adam's dream will do here and seems to be a conviction that Imagination and its empyreal reflection is the same as human Life and its spiritual repetition. . . .

(John Keats to Benjamin Bailey, November 22, 1817)

...I was purposing to travel over the north this Summer—there is but one thing to prevent me—I know nothing I have read nothing and I mean to follow Solomon's directions of 'get Wisdom—get understanding'—I find cavalier days are gone by. I find that I can have no enjoyment in the World but continual drinking of Knowledge—I find there is no worthy pursuit but the idea of doing some good for the world—some do it with their society—some with their wit—some with their benevolence—some with a sort of power of conferring pleasure and good humour on all they meet and in a thousand ways all equally dutiful to the command of Great Nature—there is but one way for me—the road lies though [for through] application study and thought. I will pursue it and to that end purpose retiring for some years. I have been hovering for some time between an exquisite sense of the luxurious and a love for Philosophy—were I calculated for the former I should be glad—but as I am not I shall turn all my soul to the latter. . . .

(John Keats to John Taylor, April 24, 1818)

F. R. LEAVIS

A Revaluation of Keats

. . . LET us consider the *Ode to a Nightingale*, commonly placed highest among the Odes, and determine in what ways, though it is not of the supreme order to which Mr Murry assigns it,[1] it is a finer and more vital thing than appreciation in terms of 'art for art's sake' can easily suggest. In memory it might at first not seem to transcend very notably Mr Symons's terms.[2] Indeed, it might on re-reading seem to be fairly describable as the work of a 'purely sensuous poet', one who was 'not troubled about his soul'; for the pang in it has little to do with moral or spiritual stress, but is, like the swooning relapse upon death, itself a luxury. 'Luxury', in fact, is a key-word in the description; 'lovely' (the beauty is of that kind), 'enchanting', 'lush' and 'exquisite' are others. One remembers the poem both as recording, and as being for the reader, an indulgence. Yet (unless the present critic's experience is exceptional) memory tends to be unjust by simplifying: re-read, the poem turns out to be subtler and finer than careless recollection suggests. And to describe and discuss this fineness there is no need to invoke the Letters; it can be discussed as a fineness of art. In fact, using this term 'art' in a way that would seem to Mr Symons right and natural, one can show Keats to be in the *Ode to the Nightingale* a better artist than Mr Symons appreciates.

'With Shelley, even though he may at times seem to become vague in thought, there is always an intellectual structure; Keats, definite in every word, in every image, lacks intellectual structure. He saw words as things, and he saw them one at a time.'

And, we may recall, A. C. Bradley, a quite different kind of critic, appears to contemplate a serious comparison between the *Ode to a Nightingale* and Shelley's *To a Skylark*.[3] Now if intellectual structure is what Shelley characteristically exhibits, the *Ode to a Nightingale* may freely be allowed to lack it. But the superiority of the Ode over *To a*

<hr>

[1] J. Middleton Murry, *Keats and Shakespeare.*
[2] Arthur Symons, *The Romantic Movement in English Poetry.*
[3] *Oxford Lectures*, p. 228.

Skylark, which beside it appears a nullity, is not merely a superiority of details ('words' and 'images' seen and felt 'one at a time'). The rich local concreteness is the local manifestation of an inclusive sureness of grasp in the whole. What the detail exhibits is not merely an extra-ordinary intensity of realization, but also an extraordinary rightness and delicacy of touch; a sureness of touch that is the working of a fine organization. The Ode, that is, has the structure of a fine and complex organism: whereas *To a Skylark* is a mere poetical outpouring, its ecstatic 'intensity' being a substitute for realization in the parts and for a realized whole to which the parts might be related.

The Ode, it has been said above, tends to suffer an unfair simplifi-cation in memory; the thought of its being 'rich to die', and the desire

> To cease upon the midnight with no pain,

tend to stand for more of it than they should. Actually, when we re-read it we find that it moves outwards and upwards towards life as strongly as it moves downwards towards extinction; the Ode is, in fact, an extremely subtle and varied interplay of motions, directed now positively, now negatively. Consider the opening stanza:

> My heart aches, and a drowsy numbness pains
> My sense, as though of hemlock I had drunk,
> Or emptied some dull opiate to the drains
> One minute past, and Lethe-wards had sunk:
> 'Tis not through envy of thy happy lot,
> But being too happy in thine happiness,—
> That thou, light-wingèd Dryad of the trees,
> In some melodious plot
> Of beechen green, and shadows numberless,
> Singest of summer in full-throated ease.

It starts Lethe-wards, with a heavy drugged movement ('drowsy', 'numb', 'dull') down to 'sunk'. The part played by the first line-division is worth noting—the difference the division makes to the phrase 'a drowsy numbness pains my sense'. In the fifth and sixth lines, with the reiterated 'happy' the direction changes, and in the next line comes the key-word, 'light-wingèd'. The stanza now moves buoyantly towards life, the fresh air and the sunlight ('shadows numberless')—the thought of happy, self-sufficient vitality provides the impulse. The common medium, so to speak, in which the shift of direction takes place with such unobtrusive effectiveness, the pervasive sense of luxury, is given explicitly in the closing phrase of the stanza, 'full-throated ease'.

Down the throat (now the poet's) flows, in the next stanza, the 'draught of vintage',

> Cool'd a long age in the deep-delved earth,

the coolness (having banished the drowsy fever) playing voluptuously against the warmth of 'the warm South'. The sensuous luxury keeps its element of the 'light-wingèd': there are the 'beaded bubbles winking at the brim'. This second stanza reverses the movement of the first; until the last two lines it moves towards life and the stirring human world,

> Dance and Provençal song and sunburnt mirth.

But the optative 'O' changes direction, as if with the changing effect (now no longer excitation) of the wine, and the stanza ends on the desire to

> leave the world unseen
> And with thee fade away into the forest dim.

The next stanza is the only one in the poem to be completely disintoxicated and disenchanted. It is notable how at the second line the tone, the manner of reading compelled on one, alters, turning from incantatory into prosaic matter-of-fact:

> Fade far away, dissolve, and quite forget
> What thou among the leaves hast never known,
> The weariness, the fever, and the fret,
> Here, where men sit and hear each other groan;
> Where palsy shakes a few, sad, last gray hairs,
> Where youth grows pale, and spectre-thin, and dies . . .

—That 'spectre-thin' is a key-word, suggesting as it does, along with 'gray', the thin unreality of the disintoxicated, unbeglamoured moments that the addict dreads.

The fourth stanza takes up the 'away' again—but not the 'fade':

> Away! away! for I will fly to thee,
> Not charioted by Bacchus and his pards,
> But on the viewless wings of Poesy . . .

—It points now, not to dissolution and unconsciousness but to positive satisfactions, concretely realized in imagination: they represent the world of 'Poesy' (for poetry was Poesy to the Keats of *Endymion* and the Odes). We have now the rich evocation of enchantment and delighted senses, and here again the touch of the consummate artist manifests itself; in the very piling up of luxuries a sure delicacy presides:

> I cannot see what flowers are at my feet,
> Nor what soft incense hangs upon the boughs,
> But, in embalmed darkness, guess each sweet
> Wherewith the seasonable month endows
> The grass, the thicket and the fruit-tree wild;
> White hawthorn, and the pastoral eglantine . . .

—the 'grass', the 'thicket' and the cool reminders of the English spring bring the needed note of freshness into the else too cloying accumulation of sweets.

And now comes a stanza that, in the simplifying memory, tends to get undue prominence:

> Darkling I listen; and, for many a time
> I have been half in love with easeful Death,
> Call'd him soft names in many a mused rhyme,
> To take into the air my quiet breath;
> Now more than ever seems it rich to die,
> To cease upon the midnight with no pain,
> While thou art pouring forth thy soul abroad
> In such an ecstasy!
> Still wouldst thou sing, and I have ears in vain—
> To thy high requiem become a sod.

—In the re-reading the force of that 'half' comes home to us: Keats is strictly only half in love with death, and the positive motion is present even in this stanza. It is present in the 'rich' of 'rich to die', a phrase that epitomizes the poem. The desire not to die appears in the thought of becoming a sod to the nightingale's high requiem and of having ears in vain, and it swells into a strong revulsion against death in the opening lines of the next stanza:

> Thou wast nor born for death, immortal Bird!
> No hungry generations tread thee down . . .

Bridges,[4] as a conscientious critic, solemnly points out the fallacy here: 'the thought is fanciful or superficial—the man being as immortal as the bird', etc. That the thought is fallacious witnesses, of course, to the intensity of the wish that fathered it. Keats entertains at one and the same time the desire to escape into easeful death from 'the weariness, the fever and the fret'—

> To cease upon the midnight with no pain,

and the complementary desire for a full life unattended by these disadvantages. And the inappropriateness of the nightingale's song as a symbol of enduring satisfaction—

[4] Robert Bridges, Introduction to Keats, *Collected Essays and Papers, Vol. I.*

> The voice I hear this parting night was heard
>   In ancient days by emperor and clown:
> Perhaps the self-same song that found a path
>   Through the sad heart of Ruth, when, sick for home,
>   She stood in tears amid the alien corn

manifests locally the complexity of the impulsions behind the poem. The regressive desire to 'cease upon the midnight' slips, it will be noticed, into the positive nostalgia represented by Ruth, the association of the two providing an interesting illustration to D. W. Harding's *Note on Nostalgia*.[5]

Bridges has also a criticism to make against the opening of the final stanza: the 'introduction', he says, is 'artificial', by which he would seem to suggest that Keats, having earlier in the Ode got his transition, managed his development, by picking up a word or a phrase already used, now mechanically repeats the closing 'forlorn' of the penultimate stanza because he can think of no better way of carrying on:

>   The same that oft-times hath
> Charm'd magic casements, opening on the foam
> Of perilous seas, in faery lands forlorn.

VIII

> Forlorn! the very word is like a bell
>   To toll me back from thee to my sole self!
> Adieu! the fancy cannot cheat so well
>   As she is fam'd to do, deceiving elf.

Actually, that the repetition has a peculiar and appropriate force is obvious, or would be if Keats had not here suffered the injury incidental to becoming 'hackneyed'. In 'faery lands forlorn'—the adjective has acquired the wrong kind of inevitability; it would but for the hackneying, but for the groove in one's mind, be seen to be, coming with the final emphasis at the end of those two glamorous lines, unexpected. It is so for Keats; he turns it over, and it becomes as he looks at it the recognition upon which the poem ends—the recognition that we, looking back, can see to have been approaching in the passage about Ruth, 'sick for home', which gives us the sickness to contemplate, not the home: even the illusion of a 'secure happiness' as something to be ecstatically, if enviously, contemplated in the nightingale is recognized to be an evanescent indulgence, belonging to the world of 'magic casements, opening on the foam of perilous seas'. The song that fades away is no longer an ecstasy, but a 'plaintive anthem'.

[5] *Determinations* (ed. by the present writer); see esp. p. 68.

The strength of the Ode, then, is far from being merely the strength of details—of things seen separately. In fact, the Ode is not only incomparably better art than Mr Symons recognizes; it is better in a way involving a relation to life that the prescription 'art for art's sake' (whatever it may mean) would not tend to encourage. On the other hand, to talk of the Ode as belonging to the same order as the work of Shakespeare's maturity is extravagantly out. It is not for nothing that it should suffer as it does in memory, or that it should not be among the poems that bear frequent re-reading. It is as if Keats were making major poetry out of minor—as if, that is, the genius of a major poet were working in the material of minor poetry. For in spite of a sublety so far transcending the powers of the not much younger poet who wrote of 'pleasant smotherings', the word for poetry (or Poesy) as practised by the poet of the Ode is still 'luxury'. The pain with which his heart aches is not that of a moral maturity, of a disenchanted wisdom born of a steady contemplation of things as they are; it is itself a luxury. The disintoxicated third stanza represents the actual upon which the poem turns its back, seeking deception. Though 'the fancy cannot cheat so well as she is famed to do', the 'sole self', plaintively yearning, can make of its very regret a sweet anodyne.

. . . The effect of . . . insisting on the Aesthete in Keats is merely to bring out still more the extraordinary force of his genius. There is, for instance, the *Ode on Melancholy*, which represents one of the most obviously decadent developments of Beauty-addiction—of the cult of 'exquisite passion' and 'finest senses'. The penalties of the addiction—the 'heart high-sorrowful and cloy'd', the 'aching pleasure . . . turning to poison', the besetting fret of transience—are themselves turned into a luxury, a peculiarly subtle drug. The Ode is, as it were, the prescription. The process is of the same order as that by which his Victorian successors ('world-losers and world-forsakers') made of their sense of defeat and impotence a kind of religious sanction—turned it into an atmosphere of religious desiderium:

> Nothing: the autumn fall of leaves.
> The whole year sets apace

—the tone pervades the work of this line from *Mariana in the Moated Grange* onwards. But Keats's *Ode on Melancholy*, a prescription for making the most of your 'sorrow's mysteries' (if you go to Lethe or make your rosary of yew-berries you drown the wakeful anguish of the soul), exhibits with peculiarly paradoxical force in the inculcation of these perverse and debilitating indulgences—it is his most Swinburnian mood—his characteristic vitality.

Paradoxical the manifestation of this vitality in the second stanza very plainly deserves to be called:

> But when the melancholy fit shall fall
> Sudden from heaven like a weeping cloud,
> That fosters the droop-headed flowers all,
> And hides the green hill in an April shroud ...

—the fresh touch when it comes is so welcome after the heavy drugged luxury of the first stanza that one does not immediately recognize the purely formal nature of the simile, which passes only by a curious sleight or bluff. Keats's melancholy attracts no doubt both the 'weeping' and the 'cloud' quite naturally; but it is not, as the poem conveys it, at all like the sudden rain that refreshes the flowers. For the 'pale forehead' of the addict it has no such virtue. Its quite opposite effect is given us at the end of the Ode:

> His soul shall taste the sadness of her might,
> And be among her cloudy trophies hung.

The sudden burst of freshness is, as it were, the vitality behind Keats's aestheticism breaking through. It leads on to the contrasting and very characteristic manifestation of vitality that follows:

> Then glut thy sorrow on a morning rose,
> Or on the rainbow of the salt sand-wave,
> Or on the wealth of globed peonies;
> Or if thy mistress some rich anger shows ...

In the strength that makes the luxury of this more than merely voluptuous we have that which makes Keats so much more than a mere æsthete. That 'glut', which we can hardly imagine Rossetti or Tennyson using in a poetical place, finds itself taken up in 'globed', the sensuous concreteness of which it reinforces; the hand is round the peony, luxuriously cupping it. Such tactual effects are notoriously characteristic of Keats, and they express, not merely the voluptuary's itch to be fingering, but that strong grasp upon the actualities—upon things outside himself, that firm sense of the solid world, which makes Keats so different from Shelley. Because of it Mr Symons is able to say of him, justly:

> 'Keats has a firm common sense of the imagination, seeming to be at home in it, as if it were literally of this world, and not of another'.

—It is, we may add, by virtue of this strength, which is at once intelligence and character, that Keats never takes his dreams for reality or (even with the Grecian urn to help him) remains lost in them. This strength is one with that which makes him put *La Belle Dame sans Merci* aside—abandoned for the Victorian romantics to find in it the essential stuff of poetry, and which makes him condemn *Isabella* as 'mawkish' and say:

> 'in my dramatic capacity I enter fully into the feeling; but in Propria Persona I should be apt to quiz it myself. There is no objection of the kind to *Lamia*—A good deal to *St Agnes Eve*— only not so glaring.[6]

The strength appears here as critical intelligence, something intimately related to the sureness of touch and grasp that makes his art in the Odes so much better than Mr Symons recognizes. It is the strength that is manifested in the extraordinary rapidity with which that art developed between *Endymion* and the *Ode to a Nightingale*.

The relation between the firmness of the art and the firm grasp on the outer world appears most plainly in the Ode *To Autumn*. Of this Mr Middleton Murry says:

> 'It is the perfect and unforced utterance of the truth contained in the magic words: "Ripeness is all".[7]

Such talk is extravagant, and does not further the appreciation of Keats. No one could have found that order of significance in the Ode merely by inspecting the Ode itself. The ripeness with which Keats is concerned is the physical ripeness of autumn, and his genius manifests itself in the sensuous richness with which he renders this in poetry, without the least touch of artistic over-ripeness.

If one might justifiably call the poem Shakespearian it would be in emphasizing how un-Tennysonian it is—how different from the decorative-descriptive verse to which we see it as pointing forward. The explicit richness of detail has its life in the vigour of the medium:

> To bend with apples the moss'd cottage-trees,
> And fill all fruit with ripeness to the core,
> To swell the gourd, and plump the hazel shells
> With a sweet kernel . . .

That 'moss'd cottage trees' represents a strength—a native English strength—lying beyond the scope of the poet who aimed to make English as like Italian as possible. So too with the unpoetical 'plump': its sensuous firmness—it introduces a tactual image—represents a general concrete vigour such as is alien to the Tennysonian habit, and such as a Tennysonian handling of the medium cannot breed. This

[6] Letter to Woodhouse, September 22, 1819.
[7] *Keats and Shakespeare*, p. 189.

English strength pervades the Ode; in another of its forms it is notably
exemplified by this, from the second stanza:

> And sometimes like a gleaner thou dost keep
> Steady thy laden head across a brook . . .

In the step from the rime-word 'keep', across (so to speak) the pause
enforced by the line-division, to 'Steady' the balancing movement of
the gleaner is enacted.

The warm richness of the poem is qualified, as with the autumnal
hint of sharpness in the air, by the last stanza, which, from 'the stubble
plains' (appropriately unvoluptuous in suggestion) onward is full of
the evocation of thin sounds—the gnats 'mourn' in a 'wailful choir',
the lambs bleat, hedge-crickets sing, the redbreast 'with treble soft'
whistles, and gathering swallows twitter in the skies.

If, then, in Keats's development from *Endymion* to the *Ode to
Autumn* we see, as we may (leaving aside for a moment the *Hyperions*)
the promise of greatness, it does not lie in any effective presence of the
kind of seriousness aspired to in *Sleep and Poetry*:

> And can I ever bid these joys farewell?
> Yes, I must pass them for a nobler life,
> Where I may find the agonies, the strife
> Of human hearts . . .

It lies rather in the marvellous vitality of the art that celebrates 'these
joys'—in the perfection attained within a limiting æstheticism. Remarkable intelligence and character are implied in that attainment. . . .

From *Revaluation: Tradition and Development in English Poetry*,
Chatto & Windus Ltd., London, 1936; George W. Stewart, Inc.,
New York, 1947, pp. 241–73. This extract was taken from pp. 378–84
and 390–4 of the original essay, which was first published in *Scrutiny*,
vol. IV, March, 1936, pp. 376–400.

CLEANTH BROOKS

Keats's Sylvan Historian

THERE is much in the poetry of Keats which suggests that he would
have approved of Archibald MacLeish's dictum, 'A poem should not
mean/But be.' There is even some warrant for thinking that the
Grecian urn (real or imagined) which inspired the famous ode was,
for Keats, just such a poem, 'palpable and mute', a poem in stone.
Hence it is the more remarkable that the 'Ode' itself differs from
Keats's other odes by culminating in a statement—a statement even of
some sententiousness in which the urn itself is made to say that beauty
is truth, and—more sententious still—that this bit of wisdom sums
up the whole of mortal knowledge.

This is 'to mean' with a vengeance—to violate the doctrine of the
objective correlative, not only by stating truths, but by defining the
limits of truth. Small wonder that some critics have felt that the unravished bride of quietness protests too much.

T. S. Eliot, for example, says that 'this line ['Beauty is truth', etc.]
strikes me as a serious blemish on a beautiful poem; and the reason
must be either that I fail to understand it, or that it is a statement which
is untrue'. But even for persons who feel that they do understand it,
the line may still constitute a blemish. Middleton Murry, who, after
a discussion of Keats's other poems and his letters, feels that he knows
what Keats meant by 'beauty' and what he meant by 'truth', and that
Keats used them in senses which allowed them to be properly brack-
eted together, still, is forced to conclude: 'My own opinion concerning the value of these two lines *in the context of the poem itself* is not
very different from Mr T. S. Eliot's.' The troubling assertion is
apparently an intrusion upon the poem—does not grow out of it—is
not dramatically accommodated to it.

This is essentially Garrod's objection, and the fact that Garrod
does object indicates that a distaste for the ending of the 'Ode' is by
no means limited to critics of notoriously 'modern' sympathies.

But the question of real importance is not whether Eliot, Murry,
and Garrod are right in thinking that 'Beauty is truth, truth beauty'
injures the poem. The question of real importance concerns beauty

and truth in a much more general way: what is the relation of the beauty (the goodness, the perfection) of a poem to the truth or falsity of what it seems to assert? It is a question which has particularly vexed our own generation—to give it I. A. Richards's phrasing, it is the problem of belief.

The 'Ode', by its bold equation of beauty and truth, raises this question in its sharpest form—the more so when it becomes apparent that the poem itself is obviously intended to be a parable on the nature of poetry, and of art in general. The 'Ode' has apparently been an enigmatic parable, to be sure: one can emphasize *beauty* is truth and throw Keats into the pure-art camp, the usual procedure. But it is only fair to point out that one could stress *truth* is beauty, and argue with the Marxist critics of the 'thirties for a propaganda art. The very ambiguity of the statement, 'Beauty is truth, truth beauty' ought to warn us against insisting very much on the statement in isolation, and to drive us back to a consideration of the context in which the statement is set.

It will not be sufficient, however, if it merely drives us back to a study of Keats's reading, his conversation, his letters. We shall not find our answer there even if scholarship does prefer on principle investigations of Browning's ironic question, 'What porridge had John Keats?' For even if we knew just what porridge he had, physical and mental, we should still not be able to settle the problem of the 'Ode'. The reason should be clear: our specific question is not what did Keats the man perhaps want to assert here about the relation of beauty and truth: it is rather: was Keats the poet able to exemplify that relation in this particular poem? Middleton Murry is right: the relation of the final statement in the poem to the total context is all-important.

Indeed, Eliot, in the very passage in which he attacks the 'Ode' has indicated the general line which we are to take in its defence. In that passage, Eliot goes on to contrast the closing lines of the 'Ode' with a line from *King Lear*, 'Ripeness is all'. Keats's lines strike him as false; Shakespeare's, on the other hand, as not clearly false, and as possibly quite true. Shakespeare's generalization, in other words, avoids raising the question of truth. But is it really a question of truth and falsity? One is tempted to account for the difference of effect which Eliot feels in this way: 'Ripeness is all' is a statement put in the mouth of a dramatic character and a statement which is governed and qualified by the whole context of the play. It does not directly challenge an examination into its truth because its relevance is pointed up and modified by the dramatic context.

Now, suppose that one could show that Keats's lines, *in quite the same way*, constitute a speech, a consciously riddling paradox, put in the mouth of a particular character, and modified by the total context of the poem. If we could demonstrate that the speech was 'in character', was dramatically appropriate, was properly prepared for—then would not the lines have all the justification of 'Ripeness is all'? In such case, should we not have waived the question of the scientific or philosophic truth of the lines in favor of the application of a principle curiously like that of dramatic propriety? I suggest that some such principle is the only one legitimately to be invoked in any case. Be this as it may, the *Ode on a Grecian Urn* provides us with as neat an instance as one could wish in order to test the implications of such a manoeuvre.

It has seemed best to be perfectly frank about procedure: the poem is to be read in order to see whether the last lines of the poem are not, after all, dramatically prepared for. Yet there are some claims to be made upon the reader too, claims which he, for his part, will have to be prepared to honour. He must not be allowed to dismiss the early characterizations of the urn as merely so much vaguely beautiful description. He must not be too much surprised if 'mere decoration' turns out to be meaningful symbolism—or if ironies develop where he has been taught to expect only sensuous pictures. Most of all, if the teasing riddle spoken finally by the urn is not to strike him as a bewildering break in tone, he must not be too much disturbed to have the element of paradox latent in the poem emphasized, even in those parts of the poem which have none of the energetic crackle of wit with which he usually associates paradox. This is surely not too much to ask of the reader—namely, to assume that Keats meant what he said and that he chose his words with care. After all, the poem begins on a note of paradox, though a mild one: for we ordinarily do not expect an urn to speak at all; and yet, Keats does more than this: he begins his poem by emphasizing the apparent contradiction.

The silence of the urn is stressed—it is a 'bride of quietness'; it is a 'foster-child of silence', but the urn is a 'historian' too. Historians tell the truth, or are at least expected to tell the truth. What is a 'Sylvan historian'? A historian who is like the forest rustic, a woodlander? Or, a historian who writes histories of the forest? Presumably, the urn is sylvan in both senses. True, the latter meaning is uppermost: the urn can 'express/A flowery tale more sweetly than our rhyme', and what the urn goes on to express is a 'leaf-fring'd legend' of 'Tempe or the dales of Arcady'. But the urn, like the 'leaf-fring'd legend' which it tells, is covered with emblems of the fields and forests: 'Overwrought,/With forest branches and the trodden weed'. When we consider the way in which the urn utters its history, the fact that it must be sylvan in both senses is seen as inevitable. Perhaps too the fact that it is a rural historian, a rustic, a peasant historian, qualifies in our minds the dignity and the 'truth' of the histories which it recites. Its histories, Keats has already conceded, may be characterized as 'tales'—not formal history at all.

The sylvan historian certainly supplies no names and dates— 'What men or gods are these?' the poet asks. What it does give is action —of men *or* gods, of godlike men or of superhuman (though not dae-monic) gods—action, which is not the less intense for all that the urn is cool marble. The words 'mad' and 'ecstasy' occur, but it is the quiet, rigid urn which gives the dynamic picture. And the paradox goes further: the scene is one of violent love-making, a Bacchanalian scene, but the urn itself is like a 'still unravish'd bride', or like a child, a child 'of silence and slow time'. It is not merely like a child, but like a 'foster-child'. The exactness of the term can be defended. 'Silence and slow time', it is suggested, are not the true parents, but foster-parents. They are too old, one feels, to have borne the child themselves. More-over, they dote upon the 'child' as grandparents do. The urn is fresh and unblemished; it is still young, for all its antiquity, and time which destroys so much has 'fostered' it.

With Stanza II we move into the world presented by the urn, into an examination, not of the urn as a whole—as an entity with its own form—but of the details which overlay it. But as we enter that world, the paradox of silent speech is carried on, this time in terms of the objects portrayed on the vase.

The first lines of the stanza state a rather bold paradox—even the dulling effect of many readings has hardly blunted it. At least we can easily revive its sharpness. Attended to with care, it is a statement which is preposterous, and yet true—true on the same level on which the original metaphor of the speaking urn is true. The unheard music is sweeter than any audible music. The poet has rather cunningly en-forced his conceit by using the phrase, 'ye soft pipes'. Actually, we might accept the poet's metaphor without being forced to accept the adjective 'soft'. The pipes might, although 'unheard', be shrill, just as the action which is frozen in the figures on the urn can be violent and ecstatic as in Stanza I and slow and dignified as in Stanza IV (the procession to the sacrifice). Yet, by characterizing the pipes as 'soft', the poet has provided a sort of realistic basis for his metaphor: the pipes, it is suggested, are playing very softly; if we listen carefully, we can hear them; their music is just below the threshold of normal sound.

This general paradox runs through the stanza: action goes on though the actors are motionless; the song will not cease; the lover cannot leave his song; the maiden, always to be kissed, never actually kissed, will remain changelessly beautiful. The maiden is, indeed, like the urn itself, a 'still unravished bride of quietness'—not even ravished by a kiss; and it is implied, perhaps, that her changeless beauty, like that of the urn, springs from this fact.

The poet is obviously stressing the fresh, unwearied charm of the scene itself which can defy time and is deathless. But, at the same time, the poet is being perfectly fair to the terms of his metaphor. The beauty portrayed is deathless because it is lifeless. And it would be possible to shift the tone easily and ever so slightly by insisting more heavily on some of the phrasings so as to give them a darker implication. Thus, in the case of 'thou canst not leave/Thy song', one could interpret: the musician cannot leave the song even if he would: he is fettered to it, a prisoner. In the same way, one could enlarge on the hint that the lover is not wholly satisfied and content: 'never canst thou kiss,/. . . yet, do not grieve'. These items are mentioned here, not because one wishes to maintain that the poet is bitterly ironical, but because it is important for us to see that even here the paradox is being used fairly, particularly in view of the shift in tone which comes in the next stanza.

This third stanza represents, as various critics have pointed out, a recapitulation of earlier motifs. The boughs which cannot shed their leaves, the unwearied melodist, and the ever-ardent lover reappear. Indeed, I am not sure that this stanza can altogether be defended against the charge that it represents a falling-off from the delicate but firm precision of the earlier stanzas. There is a tendency to linger over the scene sentimentally: the repetition of the word 'happy' is perhaps symptomatic of what is occurring. Here, if anywhere, in my opinion, is to be found the blemish on the ode—not in the last two lines. Yet, if we are to attempt a defence of the third stanza, we shall come nearest success by emphasizing the paradoxical implications of the repeated items; for whatever development there is in the stanza inheres in the increased stress on the paradoxical element. For example, the boughs cannot 'bid the Spring adieu', a phrase which repeats 'nor ever can those trees be bare', but the new line strengthens the implications of speaking: the falling leaves are a gesture, a word of farewell to the joy of spring. The melodist of Stanza II played sweeter music because unheard, but here, in the third stanza, it is implied that he does not tire of his song for the same reason that the lover does not tire of his love—neither song nor love is consummated. The songs are 'for ever new' because they cannot be completed.

The paradox is carried further in the case of the lover whose love is 'For ever warm and still to be enjoy'd'. We are really dealing with an ambiguity here, for we can take 'still to be enjoy'd' as an adjectival phrase on the same level as 'warm'—that is, 'still virginal and warm'. But the tenor of the whole poem suggests that the warmth of the love depends upon the fact that it has not been enjoyed—that is, 'warm and still to be enjoy'd' may mean also 'warm *because* still to be enjoy'd'.

But though the poet has developed and extended his metaphors furthest here in this third stanza, the ironic counterpoise is developed furthest too. The love which a line earlier was 'warm' and 'panting' becomes suddenly in the next line, 'All breathing human passion far above'. But if it is *above* all breathing passion, it is, after all, outside the realm of breathing passion, and therefore, not human passion at all.

(If one argues that we are to take 'All breathing human passion' as qualified by 'That leaves a heart high-sorrowful and cloy'd'—that is, if one argues that Keats is saying that the love depicted on the urn is above only that human passion which leaves one cloyed and not above human passion in general, he misses the point. For Keats in the 'Ode' is stressing the ironic fact that all human passion *does* leave one cloyed; hence the superiority of art.)

The purpose in emphasizing the ironic undercurrent in the foregoing lines is not at all to disparage Keats—to point up implications of his poem of which he was himself unaware. Far from it: the poet knows precisely what he is doing. The point is to be made simply in order to make sure that we are completely aware of what he *is* doing. Garrod, sensing this ironic undercurrent, seems to interpret it as an element over which Keats was not able to exercise full control. He says: 'Truth to his main theme [the fixity given by art to forms which in life are impermanent] has taken Keats farther than he meant to go. The pure and ideal art of this "cold Pastoral", this "silent form", *has* a cold silentness which in some degree saddens him. In the last lines of the fourth stanza, especially the last three lines ... every reader is conscious, I should suppose, of an undertone of sadness, of disappointment.' The undertone is there, but Keats had not been taken 'farther than he meant to go'. Keats's attitude, even in the early stanzas, is more complex than Garrod would allow: it is more complex and more ironic, and a recognition of this is important if we are to be able to relate the last stanza to the rest of the 'Ode'. Keats is perfectly aware that the frozen moment of loveliness is more dynamic than is the fluid world of reality *only* because it is frozen. The love depicted on the urn remains warm and young because it is not human flesh at all but cold, ancient marble.

With Stanza IV, we are still within the world depicted by the urn, but the scene presented in this stanza forms a contrast to the earlier scenes. It emphasizes, not individual aspiration and desire, but communal life. It constitutes another chapter in the history that the 'Sylvan historian' has to tell. And again, names and dates have been omitted. We are not told to what god's altar the procession moves, nor the occasion of the sacrifice.

Moreover, the little town from which the celebrants come is unknown; and the poet rather goes out of his way to leave us the widest possible option in locating it. It may be a mountain town, or a river town, or a tiny seaport. Yet, of course, there is a sense in which the nature of the town—the essential character of the town—is actually suggested by the figured urn. But it is not given explicitly. The poet is willing to leave much to our imaginations; and yet the stanza in its organization of imagery and rhythm does describe the town clearly enough; it is small, it is quiet, its people are knit together as an organic whole, and on a 'pious morn' such as this, its whole population has turned out to take part in the ritual.

The stanza has been justly admired. Its magic of effect defies reduction to any formula. Yet, without pretending to 'account' for the effect in any mechanical fashion, one can point to some of the elements active in securing the effect: there is the suggestiveness of the word 'green' in 'green altar'—something natural, spontaneous, living; there is the suggestion that the little town is caught in a curve of the seashore, or nestled in a fold of the mountains—at any rate, is something secluded and something naturally related to its terrain; there is the effect of the phrase 'peaceful citadel', a phrase which involves a clash between the ideas of war and peace and resolves it in the senses of stability and independence without imperialistic ambition—the sense of stable repose.

But to return to the larger pattern of the poem: Keats does something in this fourth stanza which is highly interesting in itself and thoroughly relevant to the sense in which the urn is a historian. One of the most moving passages in the poem is that in which the poet speculates on the strange emptiness of the little town which, of course, has not been pictured on the urn at all.

The little town which has been merely implied by the procession portrayed on the urn is endowed with a poignance beyond anything else in the poem. Its streets 'for evermore/Will silent be', its desolation forever shrouded in a mystery. No one in the figured procession will ever be able to go back to the town to break the silence there, not even one to tell the stranger there why the town remains desolate.

If one attends closely to what Keats is doing here, he may easily come to feel that the poet is indulging himself in an ingenious fancy, an indulgence, however, which is gratuitous and finally silly; that is, the poet has created in his own imagination the town implied by the procession of worshippers, has given it a special character of desolation and loneliness, and then has gone on to treat it as if it were a real town to which a stranger might actually come and be puzzled by its emptiness. (I can see no other interpretation of the lines, 'and not a soul to tell/Why thou art desolate can e'er return.') But, actually, of course, no one will ever discover the town except by the very same process by which Keats has discovered it: namely, through the figured urn, and then, of course, he will not need to ask why it is empty. One can well imagine what a typical eighteenth-century critic would have made of this flaw in logic.

It will not be too difficult, however, to show that Keats's extension of the fancy is not irrelevant to the poem as a whole. The 'reality' of the little town has a very close relation to the urn's character as a historian. If the earlier stanzas have been concerned with such paradoxes as the ability of static carving to convey dynamic action, of the soundless pipes to play music sweeter than that of the heard melody, of the figured lover to have a love more warm and panting than that of breathing flesh and blood, so in the same way the town implied by the urn comes to have a richer and more important history than that of actual cities. Indeed, the imagined town is to the figured procession as the unheard melody is to the carved pipes of the unwearied melodist. And the poet, by pretending to take the town as real—so real that he can imagine the effect of its silent streets upon the stranger who chances to come into it—has suggested in the most powerful way possible its essential reality for him—and for us. It is a case of the doctor's taking his own medicine: the poet is prepared to stand by the illusion of his own making.

With Stanza V we move back out of the enchanted world portrayed by the urn to consider the urn itself once more as a whole, as an object. The shift in point of view is marked with the first line of the stanza by the apostrophe, 'O Attic shape...' It is the urn itself as a formed thing, as an autonomous world, to which the poet addresses these last words. And the rich, almost breathing world which the poet has conjured up for us contracts and hardens into the decorated motifs on the urn itself: 'with brede/Of marble men and maidens overwrought'. The beings who have a life above life—'all breathing human passion far above'—are marble, after all.

This last is a matter which, of course, the poet has never denied. The recognition that the men and maidens are frozen, fixed, arrested, has, as we have already seen, run through the second, third, and fourth stanzas as an ironic undercurrent. The central paradox of the poem, thus, comes to conclusion in the phrase, 'Cold Pastoral'. The word 'pastoral' suggests warmth, spontaneity, the natural and the informal as well as the idyllic, the simple, and the informally charming. What the urn tells is a 'flowery tale', a 'leaf-fring'd legend', but the 'sylvan historian' works in terms of marble. The urn itself is cold, and the life beyond life which it expresses is life which has been formed, arranged. The urn itself is a 'silent form', and it speaks, not by means of statement, but by 'teasing us out of thought'. It is as enigmatic as eternity is, for, like eternity, its history is beyond time, outside time, and for this very reason bewilders our time-ridden minds: it teases us.

The marble men and maidens of the urn will not age as flesh-and-blood men and women will: 'When old age shall this generation waste'. (The word 'generation', by the way, is very rich. It means on one level 'that which is generated'—that which springs from human loins—Adam's breed; and yet, so intimately is death wedded to men, the word 'generation' itself has become, as here, a measure of time.) The marble men and women lie outside time. The urn which they adorn will remain. The 'Sylvan historian' will recite its history to other generations.

What will it say to them? Presumably, what it says to the poet now: that 'formed experience', imaginative insight, embodies the basic and fundamental perception of man and nature. The urn is beautiful, and yet its beauty is based—what else is the poem concerned with? —on an imaginative perception of essentials. Such a vision is beautiful but it is also true. The sylvan historian presents us with beautiful histories, but they are true histories, and it is a good historian.

Moreover, the 'truth' which the sylvan historian gives is the only kind of truth which we are likely to get on this earth, and, furthermore, it is the only kind that we *have* to have. The names, dates, and special circumstances, the wealth of data—these the sylvan historian quietly ignores. But we shall never get all the facts anyway—there is no end to the accumulation of facts. Moreover, mere accumulations of facts—a point our own generation is only beginning to realize—are meaningless. The sylvan historian does better than that: it takes a few details and so orders them that we have not only beauty but insight into essential truth. Its 'history', in short, is a history without footnotes. It has the validity of myth—not myth as a pretty but irrelevant make-belief, an idle fancy, but myth as a valid perception into reality.

So much for the 'meaning' of the last lines of the 'Ode'. It is an interpretation which differs little from past interpretations. It is put forward here with no pretension to novelty. What is important is the fact that it can be derived from the context of the 'Ode' itself.

And now, what of the objection that the final lines break the tone of the poem with a display of misplaced sententiousness? One can summarize the answer already implied thus: throughout the poem the poet has stressed the paradox of the speaking urn. First, the urn itself can tell a story, can give a history. Then, the various figures depicted upon the urn play music or speak or sing. If we have been alive to these items, we shall not, perhaps, be too much surprised to have the urn speak once more, not in the sense in which it tells a story —a metaphor which is rather easy to accept—but, to have it speak on a higher level, to have it make a commentary on its own nature. If the urn has been properly dramatized, if we have followed the development of the metaphors, if we have been alive to the paradoxes which work throughout the poem, perhaps then, we shall be prepared for the enigmatic, final paradox which the 'silent form' utters. But in that case, we shall not feel that the generalization, unqualified and to be taken literally, is meant to march out of its context to compete with the scientific and philosophical generalizations which dominate our world.

'Beauty is truth, truth beauty' has precisely the same status, and the same justification as Shakespeare's 'Ripeness is all'. It is a speech 'in character' and supported by a dramatic context.

To conclude thus may seem to weight the principle of dramatic propriety with more than it can bear. This would not be fair to the complexity of the problem of truth in art nor fair to Keats's little parable. Granted; and yet the principle of dramatic propriety may take us further than would first appear. Respect for it may at least insure our dealing with the problem of truth at the level on which it is really relevant to literature. If we can see that the assertions made in a poem are to be taken as part of an organic context, if we can resist the temptation to deal with them in isolation, then we may be willing to go on to deal with the world-view, or 'philosophy', or 'truth' of the *poem as a whole* in terms of its dramatic wholeness: that is, we shall not neglect the maturity of attitude, the dramatic tension, the emotional *and* intellectual coherence in favor of some statement of theme abstracted from it by paraphrase. Perhaps, best of all, we might learn to distrust our ability to represent any poem adequately by paraphrase. Such a distrust is healthy. Keats's sylvan historian, who is not above 'teasing' us, exhibits such a distrust, and perhaps the point of what the sylvan historian 'says' is to confirm us in our distrust.

From *The Well Wrought Urn*, Harcourt, Brace and Co. Inc., New York, Dennis Dobson, London, 1947, pp. 139-52. A footnote has been omitted. Originally published as 'History Without Footnotes: An Account of Keats's Urn', in *The Sewanee Review*, vol. LII, 1944, pp. 89-101.

KENNETH ALLOTT

Keats's *Ode to Psyche*

To Psyche is the Cinderella of Keats's great Odes, but it is hard to see why it should be so neglected, and at least two poets imply that the conventional treatment of the poem is shabby and undeserved. In his introduction to Keats (1895) Robert Bridges wrote of the 'extreme beauty' of the ode's last stanza and ranked the whole poem above *On a Grecian Urn* (though not above *On Melancholy*)[1], and Mr T. S. Eliot in an unregarded parenthesis in *The Use of Poetry and the Use of Criticism* (1933) has commented more boldly, 'The Odes —especially perhaps the *Ode to Psyche*—are enough for his [Keats's] reputation.' I sympathize with these views. *To Psyche* is neither un-flawed nor the best of Odes, but to me it illustrates better than any other Keats's possession of poetic power in conjunction with what was for him an unusual artistic detachment—besides being a remarkable poem in its own right. This may be another way of saying that it is the most architectural of the Odes, as it is certainly the one that culminates most dramatically. . . .

If we try to forget the other odes and look at *To Psyche* freshly, two immediate impressions seem normal. The first is that the poem opens badly but warms up rapidly after a weak start; the second is that, while the poem is a happy one, its tone is more exactly described if the happiness is thought of as defensive or defiant. . . . The poem moves through three stages. In the first stage (st. I, ll. 1–23) Keats sets out to praise Psyche as the neglected goddess whose sufferings and mistakes represent the inevitable conditions of human experience. She has achieved 'identity' and lasting happiness. Love is her com-panion. Keats uses the convention of a sudden vision or waking dream, which comes to him when he is wandering 'thoughtlessly', because he had learned to speak in one breath of 'the most thoughtless and happiest moments of our Lives' (Letter 183), because Spenser's mythological poetry seemed to him a kind of waking dream, and be-cause he knew that poetic experience was to be wooed by opening the mind receptively, not by concentrating its conscious powers. The vision

[1] *Collected Essays and Papers*, Vol. I.

of Psyche and 'the winged boy' in their Eden-like retreat draws some
of its richness, as I have said, from descriptions of embowered lovers
in Spenser and Milton. The tone of this first stanza is contented,
even cool, except for the touch of feeling conveyed by the repetition
'O happy, happy dove', which measure the irksome distance between the actual world and the happiness that Psyche has already
won.

The second stage of the poem spreads itself over the second and
third stanzas (ll. 24–49). Keats passes easily from the neglect of Psyche
(born as a goddess too late for the fervours of primitive worship) to
the fading and wearing out of belief in the Olympians, and then to a
nostalgic outpouring of feeling for the magnanimity of life in an age
when all nature was still 'holy' (full of the anthropologist's *mana*), all
enjoyment wholehearted, and every herdsman or shepherd the poet of
his own pleasure. The contrast is not with the age of Apuleius, but
with a present which is a twilight for poetic and mythological modes
of thought—the March of Mind has upset the balance of our natures,
making the simple enjoyment of an experience in an 'eternal moment'
an almost heroic achievement. Keats's regret embraces his own loss
of an earlier innocence. After the first quatrain of the third stanza we
have his defiance of these tendencies and changes in the age and in
himself ('Yet even in these days . . . I see, and sing, by my own eyes
inspired'). At this point the repetition of the catalogue of worship
from the ode's second stanza is a way of suggesting the poet's firmness
or obstinacy. Psyche's worship will not be skimped or abbreviated
by him in an age of unbelief.

The third and final stage of the poem consists of the fourth stanza
(ll. 50–67). Here Keats gets his second wind. The movement introduced by the emphatic

Yes, I will be thy priest . . .

represents an accession of strength. The tread is more measured than
in anything that has gone before, but there is no loss of smoothness
or pace, and the whole stanza, consisting of a single long but quite co-
herent sentence, develops its momentum quietly at first, then confi-
dently, and finally with exultation at its climax in the last quatrain.
The defiance of the third stanza gives way to confidence as Keats comes
to see how he can worship Psyche (the repetition of 'shall' and 'will' is
extraordinarily positive). Briefly, he will do so by keeping 'some un-
trodden region' of his mind as a safe refuge where Psyche or the soul
may unfold all her powers in a landscape and climate wholly benign
and friendly. The stanza constructs the remoteness and peaceful se-
clusion of a valley:

> Far, far around shall those dark-cluster'd trees
> Fledge the wild-ridged mountain steep by steep,
> And there by zephyrs, streams, and birds, and bees,
> The moss-lain Dryads shall be lull'd to sleep.

The succession of pictorial details moves in and down from the dark mountains and forests to the humming warmth of the valley floor with its streams and pastoral drowsiness, and the description comes to a focus on Psyche's refuge or shrine:

> And in the midst of this wide quietness
> A rosy sanctuary will I dress . . .

A complex image, accumulated from these details, is being offered as the equivalent of a mental state, which may be negatively defined by what it excludes. Calculation, anxiety and deliberate activity are shut out. The 'wide quietness' of the valley symbolizes a mood in which the soul will be able to breathe freely, and in which poetry, here defined as 'the wreath'd trellis of a working brain' may be coaxed to put forth its buds and bells and nameless stars. The soul is promised a rich indolence which will safeguard its natural gift for delight and restore to wholeness whatever the world beyond the mountains has broken down. In this luxurious sanctuary, a place made lovely and inviting with all the resources of a poetic imagination—and these resources are infinite, for Fancy

> . . . breeding flowers, will never breed the same . . .

—Psyche will be disposed to welcome the visits of love (whose 'soft delight' was still for Keats the soul's 'chief intensity'). Perhaps the final implications are that wholeheartedness can never be lost while Psyche is willing to welcome love in at her casement, and, less directly, that love, poetry and indolence are the natural medicines of the soul against the living death it must expect from 'cold philosophy'.

From *Essays in Criticism*, vol. VI, no. III, 1956, pp. 278–301. Reprinted in *John Keats: A Reassessment*. Edited by Kenneth Muir, Liverpool University Press, Liverpool, 1958, pp. 74–94. Three short extracts from the original essay are given here.

BERNARD BLACKSTONE

Ode to Autumn

...It is noteworthy that *To Autumn* is the only major poem of Keats that is completely unsexual. Woman as erotic object has been banished from this placid landscape. And with, all in all, what enormous relief—both for the poet and for us! For once we are absolved from peerless eyes and slippery blisses. The poem is one great sigh of relief. Thank God I'm rid of that obsession, the expanding rhythm seems to say, and can look around me again and see and enjoy the seeing! This is the real, beloved, warm world again; no longer the nightmare of wolfsbane and nightshade and death-moths. No longer, even, the pathetic fallacy of 'for ever shalt thou love, and she be fair'. For now we are back in the real world, which fades, and dies, and grows and lives again, in the undisturbable free courses of its seasons. The note is placid:

> Season of mists and mellow fruitfulness....

It is written without an exclamation mark—nor do we find one throughout the whole poem. The tone chimes with the occasion of its composition, as described in the September 21st letter to John Hamilton Reynolds:

> 'How beautiful the season is now—How fine the air. A temperate sharpness about it. Really, without joking, chaste weather—Dian skies—I never lik'd stubble-fields so much as now—Aye better than the chilly green of the Spring. Somehow a stubble-plain looks warm—in the same way that some pictures look warm— This struck me so much in my Sunday's walk that I composed upon it.'

'A temperate sharpness' in the air; but the stubble-field 'looks warm': the objective and the subjective impressions side by side. The objective, mediating the dry bracing quality of the chalkland air that Keats so much loved; the subjective, welcoming the suddenly apprehended friendliness of sundrenched spaces. It is like an emergence at the end of a long tunnel.

And all this is built not only into what I have called the expanding rhythms of *To Autumn* but into its spreading landscape, its branching and fructifying images as well. The symphonic movement of the Odes has now passed the narrows of *On Melancholy* to widen into the placid lake of this great choric song. For choric the ode is, not only in its clear insistence, in the final strophe, on the variety of natural sounds, but in its range of 'beauty's silent music' in the foison of the completed year.

The movement proceeds in Keats's now familiar pattern from the outer to the inner, from the broader 'manifestations of that beauteous life' in the field of space to the minuter organisms. The bold onward sweep of the verse catches a Handelian splendour. We are in the immediate presence of Autumn, the fourth in the sisterhood of 'sacred seasons' watched over by the maturing sun; from her and from him we descend into a lower circle, in which human and vegetable meet in the vines that run round the thatch-eaves; lower still is the circle of the orchard trees; whence we descend to the ripe gourd creeping on the ground; and finally, at the centre of this little cosmos, the clammy cell of the honey-bee. Schematic as this 'development' may seem, it is not in the least artificial, it has certainly not been thought out—and its end result forfeits nothing in immediacy, depth, or warmth. Autumn exists throughout the strophe as a *presence*, a spirit of generosity and prodigal luxuriance.

There is further development in the second strophe. Autumn herself descends into the circle of courses, into this world; now she is more or less than a presence, she is a person. To those with eyes to see, she is visible, like the goddesses of the ancient world; and with what majestic intimacy Keats presents her!

> Who hath not seen thee oft amid thy store?
>   Sometimes whoever seeks abroad may find
> Thee sitting careless on a granary floor,
>   Thy hair soft-lifted by the winnowing wind;
> Or on a half-reap'd furrow sound asleep,
>   Drows'd with the fume of poppies, while thy hook
>   Spares the next swath and all its twined flowers:
> And sometimes like a gleaner thou dost keep
>   Steady thy laden head across a brook;
>   Or by a cyder-press, with patient look,
>   Thou watchest the last oozings hours by hours.

That to my mind is the greatest personification in English poetry. It counterpoints an unbroken dignity against a delicate pathos. Hesiod and Moschus meet here. The pathos is not simply that of 'spares the next swath and all its twined flowers'—not, that is, the Miltonic regret.

It is inherent in the mother-figure herself: in her loneliness, in her patience and laboriousness and great strength and her occasional weariness. It is inherent in our knowledge that she too, with the flowers and the corn she reaps, and with the dying year, must vanish. It is for this reason, I think, that the note of tenderness here penetrates Keats's verse.

All the other odes, to a greater or lesser degree, protest and exclaim. At one point or another the note becomes a little shrill. Only *To Autumn* simply accepts. It accepts the inevitability of the cycle. And in the acceptance there is joy. Keats rejoices, first in the *relationship* of season, sun, and earth, and then in the *fruition* that stems from that relationship. Let us look back at the first strophe:

> Season of mists and mellow fruitfulness,
>   Close bosom-friend of the maturing sun;
> Conspiring with him how to load and bless
>   With fruit the vines that round the thatch-eaves run;
> To bend with apples the moss'd cottage-trees,
>   And fill all fruit with ripeness to the core;
>   To swell the gourd, and plump the hazel shells
> With a sweet kernel; to set budding more
>   And still more, later flowers for the bees,
>   Until they think warm days will never cease,
>   For Summer has o'er-brimm'd their clammy cells.

Here all is ripeness, tumescence, fruition. The cottage-trees bend, in Keats's beloved 'springy' curve, under their load of fruit, the vines hang tensely under their weight of grapes. Operative verbs are 'load', 'bend', 'swell', 'plump', 'o'er-brim': the verse itself strains under the packed sweetness and nourishment. Yet 'strain' is the wrong word— need another expression which will convey the shining tension of the gourd and the rich geometrizing of the honey-cell, growth and form in dynamic harmony. In the budding of the later flowers and the swelling of the fruit the extremes of a cycle meet: and here too are the bees, those 'little almsmen of Spring flowers', linking the four seasons and the three kingdoms, vegetative, animal and human. . . . The lines are so familiar to us from our childhood that we hardly stop to apprehend their extraordinary cosmic sweep, or to visualize, however mistily, the two great figures blending from the sky over our globe and touching with hands that bless the slowly maturing forms of life.

To Autumn presents the consummation of the process of which the Hymn to Pan in *Endymion* presented the initiation. The Hymn was concerned with seedtime, with roots, with young flowers: but it looked forward to the season of fruition. To Pan,

> Broad-leaved fig-trees even now foredoom
> Their ripen'd fruitage; yellow-girted bees
> Their golden honeycombs . . .
> . . . yea, the fresh-budding year
> All its completions.

It is a 'note' of the Keatsian vision that nothing is seen in isolation; Spring is not enjoyed purely in and for itself, but as part of the annual cycle. The whole is apprehended in the part, and the consummation in the inauguration. Everything has a use, a rôle to play in the total process; when, in the ode, 'more. And still more, later flowers' are set budding, it is 'for the bees', for the replenishment of cells which in their turn become the centres of new life. The sweet kernel of the hazel nut is for human nourishment.

The first strophe of *To Autumn* celebrates the effortless fruitfulness of nature; only in the last four lines are the bees brought in to make the link with human labour which is the theme of the second strophe. This middle section of corn and wine releases us from the cottage garden into a broad landscape of cornfields traversed by little brooks, of farms with their granaries and cider-presses. Are we in England or Italy? It doesn't matter: what matters is the 'weaving together'. The initial movement of the poem, now, is being reversed: no longer from outward inward, from the cosmic spaces to the bee's cell, but centrifugally from the human environment to the void of the sky. This is quite clear in the third and last strophe, and the poem ends with the skies in which it began:

> Where are the songs of Spring? Ay, where are they?
> Think not of them, thou hast thy music too,—
> While barred clouds bloom the soft-dying day,
> And touch the stubble plains with rosy hue;
> Then in a wailful choir the small gnats mourn
> Among the river sallows, borne aloft
> Or sinking as the light wind lives or dies;
> And full-grown lambs loud bleat from hilly bourn;
> Hedge-crickets sing; and now with treble soft
> The red-breast whistles from a garden-croft;
> And gathering swallows twitter in the skies.

The movement is undulating, in broad contrast to the strong earthward thrust of the laden trees and swollen gourds of strophe one, and to the wide horizontal sweep of the blown hair and the steady gleaner of strophe two. Here we are borne like the gnats themselves, in a wavering rhythm, resolved only in the last line which plumps for departure; and the poem achieves its final acceptance, which is the acceptance of

Winter, of seasonal death. The strophe makes no attempt to escape the note of sadness. There is nostalgia in 'Where are the songs of Spring? Ay, where are they?', though it is a gentle nostalgia. And note that Autumn has now to be *comforted*: the regret that we detected in the second strophe (where the season had given up her majestic remoteness to be incarnated as a simple peasant-woman) has reached its climax, and it is the human voice that proffers comfort: 'Think not of them, thou hast thy music too'. The touch is masterly, focussing a final pathos.

From *The Consecrated Urn*, Longmans, Green & Co., London, Barnes & Noble, New York, 1959, pp. 354–60. Ten lines and the footnotes have been omitted.

... As to the poetical Character itself, (I mean that sort of which, if I am any thing, I am a Member; that sort distinguished from the wordsworthian or egotistical sublime; which is a thing per se and stands alone) it is not itself—it has no self—it is every thing and nothing— It has no character—it enjoys light and shade; it lives in gusto, be it foul or fair, high or low, rich or poor, mean or elevated—It has as much delight in conceiving an Iago as an Imogen. What shocks the virtuous philosop[h]er, delights the camelion Poet. It does no harm from its relish of the dark side of things any more than from its taste for the bright one; because they both end in speculation. A Poet is the most unpoetical of any thing in existence; because he has no Identity —he is continually in for—and filling some other Body—The Sun, the Moon, the Sea and Men and Women who are creatures of impulse are poetical and have about them an unchangeable attribute— the poet has none; no identity—he is certainly the most unpoetical of all God's Creatures.... When I am in a room with People if I ever am free from speculating on creations of my own brain, then not myself goes home to myself: but the identity of every one in the room begins to to press upon me that, I am in a very little time anhilated —not only among Men; it would be the same in a Nursery of children. ...

(John Keats to Richard Woodhouse, October 27, 1818)

The Meaning of *Hyperion*

... To understand the full meaning of the first *Hyperion* it is expedient to read the second. In the summer of 1819 Keats was able to interpret the earlier poem with the help of what he had learned in the interval; and the second poem, precisely because it embodied this new knowledge, is both different from the first, and indispensable to its interpretation. Even during the actual composition of *Hyperion* Keats was developing rapidly, and the original conception was altered and deepened as he wrote. It is probable that the poem was conceived, at least vaguely, before the completion of *Endymion*, and that Keats's original intention was merely to fill out the old myth with poetical ornament: he trusted that the theme would acquire significance as he wrote, as had happened with *Endymion* itself. But in the year that elapsed before he began the poem he had learnt to tell a story more effectively by writing *Isabella*; he had studied and thought deeply; he had been reading Milton and Wordsworth, and from them and from Dante he had derived some valuable lessons....

As he brooded on his subject it began to acquire a contemporary significance. At the time when he began to write the first *Hyperion*, and again when he abandoned the second, Keats's mind turned to the subject of politics. 'As for Politics', he wrote in October, 1818,

> They are in my opinion only sleepy because they will soon be too wide awake—Perhaps not—for the long and continued Peace of England itself has given us notions of personal safety which are likely to prevent the re-establishment of our national Honesty—There is of a truth nothing manly or sterling in any part of the Government. There are many Madmen in the Country, I have no doubt, who would like to be beheaded on Tower Hill merely for the sake of eclat, there are many Men like Hunt who from a principle of taste would like to see things go better ... but there are none prepared to suffer in obscurity for their Country ... We have no Milton, no Algernon Sidney ... Notwithstanding the part which the Liberals take in the Cause of Napoleon I cannot

but think he has done more harm to the life of Liberty than any one else could have done.

It is clear from this that Keats disliked the reactionary government of his day; that he realized that 'a principle of taste' was not a satisfactory foundation for political action—a lesson some have still to learn; and that he disagreed with English Buonapartists such as Hazlitt.

Eleven months later, in the very letter which announced the abandonment of *Hyperion*, Keats returned to the subject of politics:

> In every age there has been in England for some two or three centuries subjects of great popular interest on the carpet: so that however great the uproar one can scarcely prophesy any material change in the government, for as loud disturbances have agitated this country many times. All civilized countries become gradually more enlighten'd and there should be a continual change for the better.

He goes on to describe how the tyranny of the nobles was gradually destroyed, and how in every country the kings attempted to destroy all popular privileges:

> The example of England, and the liberal writers of France and England sowed the seeds of opposition to this Tyranny—and it was swelling in the ground till it burst out in the French Revolution. That has had an unlucky termination. It put a stop to the rapid progress of free sentiments in England; and gave our Court hopes of turning back to the despotism of the 16(th) century. They have made a handle of this event in every way to undermine our freedom. They spread a horrid superstition against all innovation and improvement. The present struggle in England of the people is to destroy this superstition. What has rous'd them to do it is their distresses—Perhaps on this account the present distresses of this nation are a fortunate thing—tho' so horrid in their experience. You will see I mean that the French Revolution put a temporary stop to this third change, the change for the better. Now it is in progress again and I think in an effectual one. This is no contest between whig and tory—but between right and wrong.

That is why Keats hoped before he died 'to put a Mite of help to the Liberal side of the Question'.

I am not suggesting that Keats's political views found direct expression in *Hyperion,* and still less that it is an allegory of the French Revolution. But it is not fanciful to suggest that the revolutionary climate of the time contributed to, if it did not suggest, the subject of the poem. It is, on one level, a poem on Progress. Keats's desire for an England in which the progress interrupted by the Tory reaction after the revolution in France would be resumed and accelerated is reflected in the poem. The great speech of Oceanus expresses Keats's belief in progress. The Titans

> cower beneath what, in comparison,
> is untremendous might,

even as the tyrants of the world would cower before those who strove for freedom; and Saturn himself cries to Thea—

> Tell me, if thou seest
> A certain shape, or shadow, making way
> With wings or chariot fierce to repossess
> A heaven he lost erewhile; it must, it must
> Be of ripe progress.

But to discover the deeper meaning of the poem it is necessary to consider Keats's idea of progress, and the difference between the new gods and the old. It is here that Keats most obviously developed during the composition of the poem. Until he reached the end of the second book, he had intended to make Apollo merely more beautiful than Saturn and Hyperion. The speeches of Clymene and Oceanus make it clear that the law of progress envisaged by Keats was a development towards a greater perfection of beauty, in accordance with the eternal law—

> That first in beauty should be first in might;

but when he wrote the third book his conception of beauty had deepened. Already, in the first two books, Keats was groping towards the conception of Apollo expressed in Book 3. In Thea's face sorrow had made

> Sorrow more beautiful than Beauty's self;

and the 'living death' in Apollo's music had made Clymene sick 'Of joy and grief at once'. We can trace the germs of this conception to passages in *Endymion*, and to letters written after the completion of that poem. Keats had declared that 'what the imagination seizes as Beauty must be truth', and that 'Sorrow is Wisdom'; and he had spoken of his 'mighty abstract Idea . . . of Beauty in all things'—in sorrow, as well as in joy. Beauty, wisdom and sorrow he had accepted as correlatives.

Before he began the composition of *Hyperion*, Keats had been considering what he called 'Men of Achievement' and 'Men of Power'. Men of genius, he wrote,

> are great as certain ethereal Chemicals operating on the Mass of neutral intellect—but they have not any individuality, any determined Character—I would call the top and head of those who have a proper self Men of Power.

A few weeks later, he declared that the quality which 'went to form a Man of Achievement, especially in Literature', was Negative Capability. He returned to the subject in October, 1818, when he told Woodhouse that the poetical character

> is not itself—it has no self—it is everything and nothing—It has no character—it enjoys light and shade; it lives in gusto, be it foul or fair, high or low, rich or poor, mean or elevated—It has as much delight in conceiving an Iago as an Imogen. What shocks the virtuous philosopher, delights the camelion Poet.

This idea of the poetical character was partly derived from some of Hazlitt's essays in the *Round Table*; and from Hazlitt, too, Keats took the term *identity*:

> A poet is the most unpoetical of any thing in existence; because he has no identity—he is continually informing and filling some other Body—The Sun, the Moon, the Sea and Men and Women who are creatures of impulse are poetical and have about them an unchangeable attribute—the poet has none; no identity —he is certainly the most unpoetical of all God's creatures.

Keats was aware of the defects and dangers inherent in negative capability. He felt that the poet's personality was liable to be 'incoherent' and disintegrated:

> It is a wretched thing to confess; but it is a very fact that not one word I ever utter can be taken for granted as an opinion growing out of my identical nature—how can it, when I have no nature?

Tom's identity pressed upon him so much that sometimes he was obliged to go out. He became the person contemplated, and suffered with him—just as he was able to identify himself with a sparrow pecking about the gravel, or even a billiard ball:

> The identity of every one in the room begins to press upon me that I am in a very little time annihilated—Not only among Men; it would be the same in a Nursery of children.

In view of these quotations, it is noteworthy that Saturn and the other

Gods of the old dispensation possess identities. Saturn speaks of his 'strong identity', his 'real self'; but Apollo has no identity. He possesses to a supreme degree the negative capability that Keats had laid down as the prime essential of a poet. In other words, the old gods are men of power, the new gods are men of achievement. The poem describes the victory of the men of achievement. That is its primary meaning; linked with it, and almost equally important, is the account of the price that must be paid for being a man of achievement.

It is sometimes said that Keats could not finish the poem because he had expended all his powers in describing the nobility and beauty of the old gods, so that he was unable, as the poem demanded, to make the new gods superior to them. The criticism is not valid because, unless Saturn had been made noble, Oceanus genuinely wise, and Hyperion beautiful, the poem would have lost half its tragic beauty. The old order is great and beautiful—otherwise its downfall would have lacked significance. The best of the past must be conquered by the new gods. In a similar way, Blake in his poem on the French Revolution did more than justice to his representatives of the *ancien régime*.

In the first two books of *Hyperion* we are given to understand that Apollo is superior in beauty and wisdom to the old gods, but on his first appearance in Book 3 we find him overcome with sorrow. Oceanus had declared that the 'top of sovereignty' was

> To bear all naked truths,
> And to envisage circumstance, all calm.

But such a stoical submission to nature's law was not enough. Keats wished to show that sorrow could be creative: and it has even been said[1] that his whole poetic output can be regarded as an attempt to find a justification for suffering. Apollo, with no personal reasons for grief, takes upon himself the sorrows of mankind, and by so doing he is deified. He is superior to Oceanus in much the same way as Jesus, in Keats's opinion, was superior to Socrates; and he is superior to Hyperion in the same way that the poet is superior to the great heroes of which he writes. Although Keats may not at the time have been fully conscious of the identification, there is no doubt that his account of the deification of Apollo by disinterested suffering is a symbolic presentation of the 'dreamer' becoming a great poet. But the reference is wider. Keats, in his famous parable, wrote of the world, not as a vale of tears, but as a vale of soul-making; so that the deification of Apollo is symbolic of the birth of a soul in all who are thus reborn. The vale of god-making in *Hyperion* is the same as the vale of soul-making;

---

[1] Stephen Spender, *Forward from Liberalism*, p. 31.

and since, as Blake put it, 'The Poetic Genius is the true man', Keats, in describing his own conversion from dreamer to poet, was writing of the birth of the soul in all men. Apollo, though ostensibly a god, has to be deified because he represents both the poet and man:

> Knowledge enormous makes a God of me.
> Names, deeds, gray legends, dire events, rebellions,
> Majesties, sovran voices, agonies,
> Creations and destroyings, all at once
> Pour into the wide hollows of my brain
> And deify me, as if some blythe wine
> Or bright elixir peerless I had drunk
> And so become immortal.

This new knowledge Apollo learns from the silent face of Mnemosyne, who is the personification of the vision and understanding of human history, and a mirror of the inescapable suffering inherent in historical change and in the human condition itself.

This description of 'dying into life' is the conclusion of the poem. . . .

Even *Endymion* had been something more than a mythological narrative: Keats had used it to express a personal dilemma. *Hyperion,* in which he had once again 'touched the beautiful mythology of Greece', is only superficially about the ancient gods: its real subject, as we have seen, is human progress; and the new race of men imagined by the poet were not stronger or cleverer than their predecessors, but more sensitive and vulnerable—not characters, but personalities.

The weaknesses of the poem, apart from its too Miltonic style, are that Keats's narrative power is only intermittently displayed; the rhythmical impetus frequently exhausts itself at the end of a paragraph; and the fable itself is not perfectly adapted to the meaning Keats tried to impose on it. It was in an attempt to remedy these faults that he began to recast the poem in the summer of 1819.

From *Essays in Criticism,* vol. II, no. I, 1952, pp. 54–75. Reprinted in *John Keats: A Reassessment,* Edited by Kenneth Muir, Liverpool University Press, Liverpool, 1958, pp. 102–22. This extract is Section I of the original essay. Fourteen lines and the footnotes have been omitted.

D. G. JAMES

A Discussion of the
Two *Hyperions*

... THE place of Mnemosyne in the narrative requires special notice. Oceanus and Clymene merely voice the wonder and admiration they feel for the younger gods they have seen. But Mnemosyne belongs to the world both of the conquered and the conquering; she was a Titan, but is become the foster-mother of Apollo; she is both orders of deity and the transition from one to the other; she is the womb in the old order out of which the new order has been born. It is she who is at the centre of Keats's poem. Without her, Saturn and the Titans must have remained the gods of a world in perpetual infancy; and without her Apollo could not have become divine. In her the childhood of the first gods passes into the maturity of the new, the springtime of the world into its high summer and autumn. Thus, it is precisely Mnemosyne who weakens Keats's narrative and paralyses his invention. If *Hyperion* is the story of the war of the spring with the autumn, Mnemosyne strides the two worlds; she is not in time but encloses an eternity which has its spring and autumn at once. She cannot therefore appear, with any propriety, in the records of time, one figure among others; she is the totality and negation of time which includes the earlier and the later gods, and therefore stands above and over them all. Keats's main idea in writing *Hyperion* was to communicate some sense of what he had in mind in conceiving Mnemosyne; and he had also to write story. But so long as Mnemosyne occurs *in* the story, she saps away the reality of the clash of old and new gods, and the narrative fades and ceases. The idea wrecks the narrative, for the reason that the eternal as Keats appears to be conceiving it cannot occur within the temporal.

But Keats wished to write a long narrative poem; and he could do so only if the events composing his narrative formed a whole which *showed* the eternal through the representation of the temporal after the fashion of *King Lear*, as he perceived it, in which there is an 'intensity, capable of making all disagreeables evaporate, from their being in close relationship with Beauty and Truth'. *King Lear* is great and exciting drama and also, Keats believed, fulfils the highest aim of poetry, which is to make beautiful and acceptable what is terrible and tragic. To show the eternal through the creative apprehension of the temporal was what Keats wished to do and this is what he believed Shakespeare had done in *Lear*. Let his narrative in *Hyperion* then be content to represent the temporal. But if it was to do this, one thing was necessary: *he must get Mnemosyne out of the story*. Yet, such is his difficulty, that if he does so, his prime symbol and the chief means through which he is conveying the idea which animates the poem is lost to him.

There are two other points of view, very near to the last, from which it is convenient to study *Hyperion*. First, in studying the first version, we need to bear in mind that we have the advantage, not only of knowing Keats's other poetry, but of having read his letters and also, most important of all, the second version. We are able by this means to understand what was in Keats's mind, and to understand the first version in a degree not afforded by the poem itself. Few, I think, would deny that *Hyperion* is an obscure and difficult poem. We might enjoy it for its 'poetry'; but if it was all we had of Keats, it would leave a great deal unanswered. The great speech of Oceanus in the second book would necessarily arouse in us a lively curiosity to know more clearly what was in the poet's mind; and this curiosity would extend to trying to perceive how in the third book Mnemosyne is able to endow Apollo with godhead and just what is the 'knowledge enormous' to which Apollo comes by gazing on her face. Wonderful as *Hyperion* is, it is, as it stands, a baffling poem; and Keats must have known that it did not half express what was exciting his imagination.

Now we may, in the light of all we know of Keats, feel some confidence in saying that Keats desired to show what he believed was the tragic beauty of the world, and to reconcile the imagination to the suffering of the world. This suffering he seems to have believed, when seen 'under the aspect of eternity', to be 'evaporated' in a universal harmony. To see the temporal thus, in the form of eternity, and to behold the wonder of it, is godhead, the godhead of the younger gods, whose world is tragic, but because tragic, more beautiful than the world of Saturnian innocence. Mnemosyne possesses this vision and this godhead, and is able to impart it to Apollo. But all this is something which the poem at best only obscurely reveals; and the last forty lines of the third book, vital to the entire conception of the poem, which describe Apollo becoming a god through gazing on the face of Mnemosyne, not only carry us (or try to carry us) far from the excitement and pressure of narrative to a level of remote contemplative interest; they are also certainly not intelligible either in themselves or in the light of what has preceded them. Just why Apollo, on seeing in the face of Mnemosyne

> Names, deeds, gray legends, dire events, rebellions,
> Majesties, sovran voices, agonies,
> Creations and destroyings,

should become a god is not at all clear; and that Keats recognizes this, I think there can be little doubt. If this is so, Mnemosyne not only arrests Keats's narrative, in the way I [have just] tried to show, but in the enfeebled narrative which we have, she is too obscure and mysterious a figure to be a substitute for the narrative she impairs.

Secondly, it is significant that of the new gods it is Apollo who is chosen by Keats for the hero of his poem; for if Hyperion was in one sense to be the hero, he must yet, we suppose, be conclusively superseded by Apollo. Hyperion was the sun god, and so is Apollo. But Apollo is also the god of music and poetry. Equally important is the fact that Mnemosyne in Greek mythology is the mother of the Muses. Now before Apollo is made into a god, Mnemosyne says to him:

> Thou hast dream'd of me; and awaking up
> Didst find a lyre all golden by thy side,
> Whose strings touch'd by thy fingers, all the vast
> Unwearied ear of the whole universe
> Listen'd in pain and pleasure at the birth
> Of such new tuneful wonder. Is't not strange
> That thou shouldst weep, so gifted?

Apollo has a new music, to which the whole universe listens in astonishment. It is also a sad music. The music of the spring is over. Yet

> . . . not for this
> Faint I, nor mourn nor murmur; other gifts
> Have followed; for such loss, I would believe,
> Abundant recompense. For I have learned
> To look on nature, not as in the hour
> Of thoughtless youth; but hearing oftentimes
> The still, sad music of humanity,
> Nor harsh nor grating, though of ample power
> To chasten and subdue.

The lines of Wordsworth come naturally to the mind. This is the 'new tunefulness' of Apollo. His imagination can hear and his art catch that sad music of humanity and find it neither harsh nor grating.

Apollo then is at once god and poet. His godhead is also his poethood. He comes to see as a god sees, as it is the high and final achievement of the poet to see, as Shakespeare (so Keats believed) came to see, and as Keats wished to see. The poet may come to the divine vision such as a god has. If this is so, *Hyperion* is by way of being an exposition of what poetry, in its highest reaches, consists in; Keats is trying to tell us the aim and object of the poet. But what place, we ask, has this intention in a narrative poem? Can a narrative poem suitably undertake such a purpose? A narrative poem, or, it may be, a play, should in Keats's view so present plot and situation as to show human life 'as a God sees' it, to show 'the disagreeables evaporating from their being in close relationship with Beauty and Truth'. But instead of doing this, Keats is using his poetry to explain that this is what poetry ought to do. He is writing about the aim of poetry, instead of executing it. It is not enough for him to speak of actions and events shown to Apollo in the face of Mnemosyne; he should show, to his readers, the face of Mnemosyne in action and event. It is not enough for him to speak of the new sad tunefulness of Apollo; he must make that music sound in the ears of his readers.

Now if the analysis I have attempted is near the mark, we can sum up the position in this way. *Hyperion* is a poem in which narrative and contemplation, story and symbol, myth and meaning clash with and annul each other. . . .

We must now consider the second *Hyperion*, which he had composed in the summer. Once again we have to discuss a fragment, and a shorter fragment than the last. In the first version, Keats had failed to unite idea and narrative. In the second version, he plays boldly and simply *sunders* them. He was aware that in the first version he had not been able to make the narrative bear the load of his meaning; and he now begins by telling us what it is all about and why he wants to tell this narrative. He will explain to us. In the first version, the speech of Oceanus leaves us cloudy and uncertain, and the transformation of Apollo into a god through gazing on the face of Mnemosyne is much too mysterious. He must now in his second version make these things clear—if he can. But how can he explain? How can he make the narrative, as it were, speak to us and explain itself? Even if he is determined to sunder, as I have said, idea and narrative, the exposition of the idea on the one hand, and the narrative on the other, must be formally related to each other. He solves this problem by taking Mnemosyne out of the narrative and by introducing himself into the poem. Mnemosyne will show the story of the warring gods in a vision, and will act as chorus and commentary upon it; Keats will be the audience. But even so, how are Keats and Mnemosyne to come together? There is only one way: in a dream of the poet's mind. Mnemosyne will be a figure in his dream; and the story, shown in vision by Mnemosyne, will be a vision within a dream. This scheme is pretty complicated and does not augur well for the success of the poem.

But at the outset it gives Keats a great advantage. He can now both tell the story (however he may work it out) and explain it. But this advantage is, another way, a dead loss. For it is Keats's acknowledgement of his failure to make the story self-luminous, to fuse thought and image, the universal and the particular.

It will be recalled that I said three things of the first *Hyperion*: (1) that it was necessary to remove Mnemosyne from the narrative; (2) that Mnemosyne is, in any case, too mysterious and unexplained; (3) that Apollo is a disguise for Keats in particular and poetry in general. In the second version, Keats has tried to do something in respect of all three, which are closely bound up with one another. In the first place, Mnemosyne is taken out of the narrative and is now shown for what she is, a figure out of time. She is now the Eternal Mother of the Muses, to whom Keats can go in this version, as Apollo went in the former. Then, having regard to the third point before speaking of the second, the Apollo of the first version has become the Keats of the second; so that if Mnemosyne has stepped out from the narrative of the gods, so has Apollo, now in the form of Keats. But in this case, were Mnemosyne and Apollo to appear in the story which Mnemosyne will show in vision to Keats? To this question, so far as Apollo is concerned, we cannot give a reply; so far as the second version extends, Apollo is not introduced and we have no means of ascertaining what Keats thought to do. Certainly, this must have presented him with a difficulty, since the poet of the first canto has, it seems, taken on the role of Apollo, as the one who derives 'knowledge enormous' from the vision of the face of Mnemosyne. But so far as the question relates to Mnemosyne, we are in a better position to make reply; and the answer reveals with great clearness, I think, one at least of the difficulties which confronted Keats in the making of the second version.

In the first canto the poet finds himself in dream confronted by Mnemosyne (usually in this version, but not always, called Moneta —she is sometimes called Mnemosyne, as in canto 1, l. 331); he is weighed down by the world's pain and speaks to the goddess who uncovers her face. Her face is described in a passage which is famous. Keats asks to see and understand the 'high tragedy' which

> . . . could give so dread a stress
> To her cold lips, and fill with such a light
> Her planetary eyes; and touch her voice
> With such a sorrow?

The reply to this is a vision of Saturn and Thea, as we see them in the beginning of the first version. Mnemosyne explains who they are (ll. 332-5). Then the poem goes on to further description of Saturn and Thea in their despair. Then, at l. 384, we come to:

> A long awful time
> I look'd upon them: still they were the same;
> The frozen God still bending to the Earth,
> And the sad Goddess weeping at his feet.
> Moneta silent. Without stay or prop
> But my own weak mortality, I bore
> The load of this eternal quietude,
> The unchanging gloom and the three fixed shapes
> Ponderous upon my senses a whole moon.

We have here an uncomfortable feeling that Moneta-Mnemosyne is vaguely a part of the vision as well as a figure outside it who is showing and explaining it to the poet. And in another part (canto 1, l. 226) she describes herself as

> . . . left supreme
> Sole priestess of his [Saturn's] desolation;

so that, even in the second version, she belongs, vaguely, to the narrative of the gods. But she is also an eternal figure, the mother of poets, here conversing with Keats. Now this is clearly a clumsy arrangement, and again, is bound to make Keats's progress in this second version very difficult. And if he was in this difficulty with Mnemosyne, how would the poet who converses with Mnemosyne be connected with Apollo— if Apollo was to appear at all? Thus it is, that if Mnemosyne in the narrative was an embarrassment to Keats, she is also an embarrassment out of it.

To come now to the second of the three points around which this discussion is turning, we see that the second version at least gives Keats the chance of showing us more clearly what he intended by Mnemosyne. The subjective framework of the second version makes possible what the epic and high objective manner of the first rendered very difficult, if not impossible. Released, by his new procedure, from the pressure of the demands of narrative, he can in favourable and leisured circumstances describe at length the face of Mnemosyne, which he did not do in the first version. This passage, in the first version, would have been too remote from action, too rarefied and mystical. Here it is more natural, after the converse Keats and the goddess have had together. Moreover, Keats does not regard the face of Mnemosyne, as he has described it, as satisfying his burning curiosity; and he leads on to the narrative of the wars of the gods by offering the coming story as an explanation of the stress of her lips, the sorrow of her words, and the light of her planetary eyes. The whole story to come will serve the purpose of providing fuller apprehension of the face of Mnemosyne; for it is she, in the second as in the first version, who is central, though in the first she is set in the story and in the second outside it. For in both versions she is the mother of all poets, in her sorrow and suffering and luminous serenity. . . .

When we compare the two versions, the outstanding point of contrast is this. The first version is an attempt at high narrative, in a more or less epic manner. Keats was setting out to use his powers of invention. He desired a long, objective poem. In this he fails. He falls back on something less ambitious, reduces his style from anything approaching the epic level, and writes in 'cantos' instead of 'books'; but above all, he writes something professedly subjective, which is a dream in his own mind, and which is indeed frankly about himself and about poetry. 'Invention' has been defeated; and this not only in the first version, but even in the lesser degree required in the second. In adopting the second mode of procedure, Keats obtained, as we have seen, certain advantages; but these advantages also brought complications. In any case, Keats was aware that in the second version he was attempting something intrinsically inferior; for in large measure he had sacrificed objective invention, and his heart could not be in what he was doing in the same degree. This is all the more to be regretted because more than any other member of the Romantic group, Keats saw that what was required was the flowing out of the imagination to apprehend event and circumstance and to show them creatively. He wished to get beyond lyric and subjectivity. He did not wish to talk, but to reveal; not to say, but to show. In *Hyperion,* we may say that the Romantic movement made its greatest effort to create, to go beyond itself into the world. But tragically, like his own Saturn, Keats could not create; Mnemosyne, the mother of the great poets, of whom Keats is one, had failed him. He might, no doubt, have gone on to a finish, as Shelley had done in *Prometheus.* But he chose not to; and his choice was an act of high criticism. The Keats of *Isabella* may, as Arnold said, have lacked criticism. But *Isabella* is no criterion by which to judge Keats. He died in his twenty-seventh year; and his last year was filled with ill health and bitter unhappiness. Yet his mind, in its quality and range, in its passionate desire for what is ideal, in its exquisite and balanced scepticism, in its acceptance, in serenity, of sorrow and suffering, is wonderful to contemplate; and not least wonderful is his failure in what was to be his greatest and most ambitious work. He set himself high standards, in a plenitude of critical power; and he knew what was failure and what was not. . . .

The reader will have noticed that in what I have said of *Hyperion,* I have interpreted Mnemosyne as symbolizing a perfection and harmony in all existence—an interpretation in accordance with that second strain of speculation and with that second interpretation of 'Beauty is Truth' which we have noticed earlier. This interpretation appears, in the light of all we know, to suit the poem most adequately. I need not again comment on the passage in which Keats describes the face of Mnemosyne as it is disclosed to him. It shows a union of extreme suffering with great serenity. As we have seen, on beholding the countenance of the goddess, Keats desires to know what 'high tragedy' lies behind, in the 'dark secret Chambers' of her mind. If the interpretation by which we have proceeded is correct, Keats, using Mnemosyne as a symbol, sees the world of human experience as a 'high tragedy' which is somehow serene and beautiful. Our imagination of Mnemosyne is, I think, best helped by the thought of Cordelia. Indeed it is exceedingly likely that Keats's own imagination was thus helped.

> Patience and sorrow strove
> Who should express her goodliest. You have seen
> Sunshine and rain at once; her smiles and tears,
> Were like a better way; those happy smilets
> That play'd on her ripe lip seem'd not to know
> What guests were in her eyes; which parted thence,
> As pearls from diamonds dropp'd. In brief,
> Sorrow would be a rarity most belov'd,
> If all could so become it.

In lines which follow, Shakespeare appears almost to endow Cordelia with divine attributes:

> . . . there she shook
> The holy water from her heavenly eyes.

Then, after she and Lear have been defeated and captured, these are the words (they are the only words) she speaks:

> We are not the first
> Who, with best meaning, have incurr'd the worst.
> For thee, oppressed King, I am cast down;
> Myself could else out-frown false fortune's frown. . . .

Now Cordelia, it is true, is set within a tragedy; unlike Mnemosyne, she is a suffering mortal. But it is precisely by the achievement of serenity within the tragic sequence that she rises above it and partakes of what Keats symbolizes in Mnemosyne. Moreover, what Mnemosyne was and symbolized, Keats wished to be, as a poet and as a man. Mnemosyne is indeed a goddess, but in one respect she stands for what Keats hoped the human soul might come to, acceptance of a tragic lot and the attainment of serenity in it, through which what is tragic is also seen as beautiful.

Now I have already said that this 'speculation' of Keats is one which the facts of our experience press against with great force. We may, and perhaps ought to, be able to come to the serenity in suffering of which Keats speaks; but we cannot come to the reconciliation with this world of which he speaks. I think it very probable that when Shakespeare was writing *Lear* some such 'speculation' as animated Keats animated him also, at least to some extent. But Shakespeare gave his 'speculation' no mercy. He did not seek to spare it; and he loaded the play with suffering, both physical and mental, which goes beyond anything in his other plays. And we see, in *Lear*, seeping in unobserved, obscurely determining the choice of phrase and incident, a mode of perception which cannot spring from *this* 'speculation', but which arises from another. Lear comes out of the storm into the redeeming love of Cordelia in her superhuman beauty; she receives back the Prodigal, who has fallen from and rejected her, with words that echo the familiar story:

> And wast thou fain, poor father,
> To hovel thee with swine and rogues forlorn,
> In short and musty straw?

Then she is hanged from a beam, and darkness descends on us; but being what we are, it cannot fail to be a darkness of waiting and expectation.

Now when we read the lines in *Hyperion*—

> But for her eyes I should have fled away.
> They held me back, with a benignant light,
> Soft-mitigated by divinest lids
> Half closed, and visionless entire they seem'd
> Of all external things—they saw me not,
> But in blank splendor beam'd like the mild moon,
> Who comforts those she sees not, who knows not
> What eyes are upward cast—

we cannot fail to ask, Who is Mnemosyne,[1] this suffering and serene, benignant and comforting? If she is benignant she is no mere cosmic tragedy, however harmonious and sublime; and if she gives comfort, she cannot do so as a high impersonal order in which our sorry lives are but contributions to a grand synthesis. We might well curse such a world beyond Good and Evil in place of loving it. But as Keats sees Mnemosyne, as a symbol of the world, there are in her face values of the spirit which no naturalistic scheme can place at the centre of its universe. To be benignant is to be kind and gracious to inferiors; and the benignancy of Mnemosyne is such as is not warranted by Keats's naturalistic speculation, however noble. The awe and worship which Keats extends to her is no mere love of an impersonal order; it

---

[1] She is, of course, for the greater part, called Moneta in the second version.

is warmed with a love which is saturated by our values. There is then, another 'speculation' present in this passage; and it is a 'speculation' by no means foreign to Keats and which we have studied in his letters. In *Lear*, Albany says that if

> . . . the heavens do not their visible spirits
> Send quickly down to tame these vile offences,
> It will come,
> Humanity must perforce prey on itself,
> Like monsters of the deep.

No doubt in this Shakespeare was 'speculating'. And through Keats's apprehension of Mnemosyne there ran, not explicitly perhaps, a 'speculation' or perception of the Divine as bearing the woes of the world, and through its labour of vicarious suffering, giving comfort and light to perplexed humanity. We can hardly read the lines which portray the countenance of Mnemosyne without seeing the face of the agonized Christ. Christianity has never said that our hearts can be reconciled to the suffering of the world—it must always remain mysterious to us; it has never said that it may be justified by an 'Absolute' to which it is callously condemned to contribute. Instead, Christianity has said that our imaginations can endure the huge reality of evil and pain only when we see it freely endured and borne by God himself. I suggest that something of the sense of this has passed into Keats's lines. . . . And when Apollo, in the first version, is shown in his passage into deity after beholding the face of Mnemosyne, Keats can only describe what he undergoes as 'dying into life', a phrase in which, better perhaps than in any other, the Christian life is expressed.

It would be as absurd to call Keats a Christian as to use the word for Shelley. He was repelled by Christian dogma as greatly as Shelley. 'It is to be lamented,' he said of Christ, that his history '. . . was written and revised by Men interested in the pious frauds of Religion.' Then he adds that 'through all this I see splendour' (using a word he employs in describing Mnemosyne). Later on, the Romantic movement (if we can allow ourselves to speak thus loosely) will see Christian dogma very differently. But to Shelley and Keats it was anathema. But this did not mean and could not mean that their imaginations were not shot through with ways of feeling and perceiving which could not have been possible to them had they not been reared in a civilization which owed its existence to Christianity.

From *The Romantic Comedy*, OUP, London, 1948, Part II, 'Purgatory Blind' [An essay on Shelley and Keats]. This extract has been taken from pp. 138–50 of the original essay. Title supplied by the editor.

SELECT BIBLIOGRAPHY

POEMS

H. W. Garrod (ed.). *The Poetical Works of John Keats*. London and New York: Oxford University Press, 2nd ed., 1958. This is the standard text.

Ernest de Sélincourt (ed.). *The Poems of John Keats*. London: Methuen, 1905; revised ed., 1926; reprinted, 1954. This earlier edition is still useful.

Roger Sharrock (ed.). *John Keats: Selected Poems and Letters*. London and New York: Oxford University Press, 1964. This is a good selection of poems together with some letters and an excellent introduction.

There are several paperback editions and selections of Keats's poems. The Everyman paperback, edited by Gerald Bullet (Everyman's 101, Dutton) is particularly good.

LETTERS

M. B. Forman (ed.). *The Letters of John Keats*. 2 vols. London and New York: Oxford University Press, 4th ed., 1952.

Frederick Page (ed.). *Letters of John Keats*. London and New York: Oxford University Press, 1954. An excellent and inexpensive selection.

H. E. Rollins (ed.). *The Letters of John Keats 1814–1821*. 2 vols. Cambridge, Mass.: Harvard University Press, 1958. This is the definitive edition.

H. E. Rollins (ed.). *The Keats Circle*. 2 vols. Cambridge, Mass.: Harvard University Press, 2nd ed., 1965. These are the letters of Keats's family and friends written during and after his lifetime.

BIOGRAPHY

Walter Jackson Bate. *John Keats*. Cambridge, Mass.: Harvard University Press, 1963.

Aileen Ward. *John Keats: The Making of a Poet*. New York: Viking, 1963.

Both of these books are full and detailed and will replace earlier biographies. Aileen Ward's is probably the better of the two and is more pleasing and readable in its style.

STUDIES OF KEATS

There are several works that relate the events of Keats's life and his reading of literature to the process of composition of his own poems. The best of these biographical-critical works are the following:

Bernard Blackstone. *The Consecrated Urn.* New York: Barnes & Noble, 1959. His brilliant flashes of insight compensate for the rather wearisome comparisons with Erasmus Darwin and others.

Robert Gittings. *The Living Year.* London: Heinemann, 1954. Deals in detail with Keats's life and poetry in that remarkable year September, 1818—September, 1819.

J. Middleton Murry. *Keats and Shakespeare.* London and New York: Oxford University Press, 1925. Marks a turning point in Keats studies. Passionate and persuasive, often wildly wrong, but always stimulating.

E. C. Pettet. *The Poetry of John Keats.* London and New York: Cambridge University Press, 1957. Sensitive and helpful.

M. R. Ridley. *Keats' Craftsmanship.* New York: Russell & Russell, 1952; paperback edition, Lincoln: University of Nebraska Press, 1963. Concentrates mainly on the composition of *The Eve of St. Agnes.*

GENERAL CRITICAL STUDIES

Edmund Blunden. *John Keats.* New York: Collins, Rev. ed., 1954. Short but good.

C. M. Bowra. *The Romantic Imagination.* London and New York: Galaxy Books, Oxford University Press, 1961. (Chapters I, VI, and XII.)

Walter H. Evert. *Aesthetic and Myth in the Poetry of John Keats.* Princeton, N. J.: Princeton University Press, 1964. Some interesting arguments, but a style that lapses into pretentious wordiness.

H. W. Garrod. *Keats.* London and New York: Oxford University Press, 2nd ed., 1939.

D. G. James. *The Romantic Comedy.* London and New York: Oxford University Press, 1945. (Part II. Purgatory Blind.)

D. G. James. *Scepticism and Poetry.* London: Allen and Unwin, 1937. (Chapter VI. Adam's Dream.)

Earl R. Wasserman. *The Finer Tone.* Baltimore, Md.: Johns Hopkins University Press, 1953. Has a chapter on *La Belle Dame Sans Merci,* a poem which escapes the attention of many critics. Tends to remark too laboriously on the obvious.

ESSAYS

These collections of essays by different hands need to be used with discretion. Within each collection the quality of the essays ranges from the brilliant to the dull and perverse.

Meyer H. Abrams (ed.). *English Romantic Poets.* New York: Galaxy

Books, Oxford University Press, 1960.

W. J. Bate (ed.). *Keats: Twentieth Century Views*. Englewood Cliffs, N. J.: Prentice Hall, 1964.

Kenneth Muir (ed.). *John Keats: A Reassessment*. New York: Lounz, 1958.

C. D. Thorpe, C. Baker, and B. Weaver (eds.). *The Major English Romantic Poets: A Symposium in Reappraisal*. Carbondale: Southern Illinois University Press, 1957.

Four unusual essays of particular interest to honors students are the following:

Kenneth Burke. 'Symbolic Action in An Ode by Keats' in *A Grammar of Motives*. Englewood Cliffs, N. J.: Prentice Hall, 1945. (*The Grecian Urn*.)

H. M. McLuhan. 'Aesthetic Pattern in Keats's Odes' in *The University of Toronto Quarterly*, vol. XII, 1942-3. (The *Nightingale*.)

Allen Tate. 'A Reading in Keats' in *On the Limits of Poetry*. New York: New York: William Morrow, 1948. (The *Nightingale*.)

Katharine M. Wilson. Chapter IV of her book *The Nightingale and the Hawk*, New York: Barnes & Noble, 1965. An interpretation of the *Nightingale* based on Jung's psychology.

QUOTATIONS FROM LETTERS

The quotations from letters that appear at the end of essays in this book are taken, with their original punctuation and spelling, from:

The Letters of John Keats, 1814–1821. Ed. Hyder Edward Rollins. 2 vols. Cambridge, Mass.: Harvard University Press, 1958.

The Further Letters of Gerard Manley Hopkins. Ed. Claude Colleer Abbott. London and New York: Oxford University Press, 1938.